SUE CHRISTENSEN

MAKING A SIX FIGURE INCOME ON YOUR TERMS

Essential Life Balance for a Highly Successful and Personally Satisfying Real Estate Career

Copyright © 2002 by Sue Christensen

All rights reserved. No part of this work may be reproduced or transmitted in any form by any means, electronic or mechanical, including photocopying and recording, or by any information storage or retrieval system, except as may be expressly permitted by the 1976 Copyright Act or in writing by the publisher.

Requests for such permissions should be addressed to:
Destiny Publishing Co.
2675 West Fanbrook Road
Tucson, Arizona 85741
www.earnsixfigures.org

Christensen, Sue
    Six Figure Income

Cover: Graphics by Manjari
Layout: J. L. Saloff
Fonts: Century Schoolbook & Capitals

ISBN: 0-9723683-0-2

To my Angels on Earth:

Judy, my port in the storm, Mom, Barb, Julie, Sue, and Iris for your constant love and support, and to my beloved sons, Pat and Tim who bring true meaning to being *booked solid*.

For More Information write or call:

Destiny Publishing Co.
2675 West Fanbrook Road
Tucson, Arizona 85741
520-293-7676
sue@EarnSixFigures.org

or visit Sue's website at:

www.EarnSixFigures.org

Six Figure Income

Table of Contents

Introduction

Mental Preparation The Mindset Of Success
Goals, Dreams, Expectations 3
Writing Your Own Life Script 4
Examining the Why (I) 4
Examining the Why (II) 5
Goal Planning Guide 5
Everything Has a Price 6
Ask Yourself (I) 6
Ask Yourself (II) 7
The Impact of Our Belief System 8
Ask Yourself (III) 8
See Yourself Successful 10
Make A Treasure Map 11
Affirmations 12

Master-Minding
The Master Mind Alliance 15
The Power of Two... Or More 16
Master Mind Group Discussions 16
Surrounding Yourself With Productivity 18
Creating Your Own Master Mind Group 19
Straight From The Masters 19

The Foundation of Your Business
Business Systems 23

Working From A Business Plan
Treat it Like a Business 23
Begin At The End / Example 1 24
The Numbers 25
Don't Over-Complicate 26
Begin At The End / Example 2 26
Managing Sixty Transactions 27

The 'P' Word: Prospecting
Telling the Whole World 29
Confidence = Knowing What to Say 30
Your Million Dollar ABCs 31
Go Three Deep 31
Lesson From The Masters 32
Practice Makes Perfect 33
Scripting FSBO's and Expireds 34

Table of Contents

The Call That's Most Critical 35
Door-Knocking Without Doors 36
How Can You Make This Work For You? 37
'Door-Knocking' Everywhere You Go 39
Overview Of The Goals Of Prospecting 41
Daily Prospecting Log 42

Taking Control Of Your Time

The Magic of The Five Day Week 45
Be Responsible 47
Don't Over-complicate It. 48
Work isn't Life, it's what we do to Fund Life 49
When the Values are clear, the Decisions are Easy. 50
Setting Our Own Boundaries 50
See Yourself As A Professional 51
Helping Others Adjust Their Thinking 51
The Three Keys To A 'Day Off' 52
The 'F' Word in Real Estate: Floor Time 54
Do You Have A Job, Or A Business? 54
'No Open House' Alternative Marketing 54
135 Days and 365 Nights Off 55
Your Model Day (I) 56
Example Model Day 56
Your Model Day (II) 57

Running A Smooth Operation Delegation And Outsourcing

Working With An Assistant 62
Let 'George' Do It. 63
Getting People To Read It 64
Avoiding Panic Promotions 65
Hiring And Training An Assistant 65
You Need An Assistant 67
Assistant's Job Description 68
How Do I Find This Person? 71
Reviewing the Resumes 71
The First Interview 72
Making The Cut 72
The First Interview 73
The Second Interview 74
Checking the Enthusiasm Level 76
Orientation 76
Get Out Of The Way 77
Hands-on Training 78
New Listing Check List 79
Escrow File Check List 81

# Six Figure Income

Table of Contents

    Assistant Orientation Tips 82
    Don't Make These Hiring Mistakes 83

Systems For Everything
    The Prospecting System 85
    The Follow Up System 87
    Title Company Folder Items 88
    Built-in Price Reduction Strategy 89
    Be Strong On Pricing 89
    Qualify! Qualify! Qualify! 90
    Avoid The Deadly Three 91
    The Buyer Interview 92
    Buyer Information 93
    Safety Precautions 95
    Another Look At Qualifying 97
    Qualify Everyone Working With Your Client 97
    Lifetime Value of A Satisfied Client 98

Putting Your Plan Into Action
    Know Your Market 99
    MLS Market Place Check List 100
    Fill The Front Of the Week First 101
    Time For Action 102

The Pre-Listing Package and Listing Appointment
    What's In A Pre-Listing Package? 105
    The Pre-Listing Package 105
    Show Time: The Listing Appointment 106
    Twelve Important Questions To Ask Your Agent 106
    Seller Information 108
    Be Prepared To Walk Away 109
    Listing Information 111

Making Yourself Famous Providing Legendary Service
    Memorable Housewarming Gifts 116
    Specially Delivered Thank Yous 116
    Staying In Touch 117
    Uncommon Courtesies 118
    Client Appreciation Events 119
    You're Invited! 120
    Say Thank You With A Photo 120
    More Ideas For Client Appreciation Events 121
    Even More Ideas For Client Appreciation Events 122
    Still More Ideas For Client Appreciation Events 123
    Following Up The Easy Way 125

TABLE OF CONTENTS

PERSONAL PROMOTION
Standing Out in The Crowd 127
Developing a Theme for Your Promotion Campaign 128
Let Your Imagination Go Wild! 130
Uses For Your Promotional Theme 130
Blow Your Own Horn 131
Using Your Theme For Mailings 132
Consistency In Mailings 132
What's In A Name? 133
Synchronize Your Promotion Campagain 134
Be Seen Everywhere 135
Keys To An Effective Ad 135
Taking Sponsorships To A New Level 136
'Photogenic' Sales 136
Giving Something Back 138

IMPLEMENTING IDEAS
Sorting and Prioritizing 139
The Top Twelve System 140
The Larger-than-Life Things 141
Become A Stand Out 141
Make Decisions That Fit The Big Picture 142
Letting Them Know 143
Food Drive/Holiday Toy Collection 144
Zero-Based Advertising 145

THE REALITIES OF LIFE BALANCE THE BIG PICTURE: KEEPING ALL THE BALLS IN THE AIR
Delegation Re-visited 150
Delegation At The Office 151
Preferred Client Referral Form 152
Delegation of Personal Chores 153
Delegation At Home 153
Have Systems At Home, Too 154
Hiring A Sign Contractor 156

TIME-SENSITIVE RESPONSIBILITIES
Top Priority 157
Deliver Your Greatest Strength 158
Just How Many Exceptions Are There? 158
Use Common Sense 159

SIX FIGURE INCOME

TABLE OF CONTENTS

EXPERIENCE = BETTER PROFITABILITY
Don't Be A Rookie Very Long 161
The Fifty Pound Fish 161
Keeping It Simple 162
Turning Up The Heat 163
Take Your Commitment Seriously 164
100% Commissions 164
Maintaining Good Office Relations 165

RE-EVALUATION: IS THIS WHAT YOU REALLY WANT?
A Second Look 167
Compare The Numbers 168
Goals Re-Evaluation 168
Everything Has A Price 169
Reviewing The Components Of Production 170
Tracking By The Numbers 171
Stay Focused On Mindset 172
Review Your Business Plan Weekly 172
Gifts For All Reasons 175

REVOLUTIONIZING RETAIL SALES
The Jewelry Broker 175
King of Dreams 176
Especially For Her 176
Become A 'Hero Maker' 178
Jewelry Broker's Action Plan 179
Sending Manageable Quantities: 180
Initial Contact 180
Phone Script for the Follow-Up Calls: 181
Phone Script 181
Department Store Associate's Action Plan 182
The Appointment 182
General Tips 183

HOW LIFE BALANCE REFLECTS THE WHY
Re-Focus on Mindset 185
The Individuality of Spending Habits 186
What Makes Your Heart Sing? 187
Smelling the Roses. . . Really. 187
Help From The Experts 189
Acknowledgements: 191

ABOUT THE AUTHOR

> With the work effort and belief system of success and full expectation of high achievement, there are literally no limits to what we can accomplish.

Introduction

Success cannot be achieved in any field without a proper blend of mindset and work ethic. There are many factors that need to be incorporated, but these two elements are the basis of achievement. Superior business skills, dedicated commitment to the daily application of sound practices, and good work habits are absolutely essential.

In the field of sales, prospecting is without question the single element that will determine the level of production. Because it is such an integral part of building and sustaining a successful sales career, it affects and is essential to every other element of the business. It is literally the foundation of all else that follows and is, therefore, present in some form in nearly every chapter of this book.

The same is true of mindset. The belief of what we can or cannot do, will determine what, in fact, we do. The power of mindset in business is often overlooked, and is actually quite extraordinary. If our life experience and upbringing is such that we are constantly surrounded by people who live simple lives without achievement, we can still go on to great achievement if, indeed, we *believe* we can, if the mindset that is present in all things promotes the *expectation* of success. Because of its profound impact on our lives, and all that we do, mindset and its application to the many essential elements of a successful sales career, will also be present in nearly every chapter of this book.

This book is about a blending of mindset and work ethic into every other element of the daily habits and practices that comprise a successful sales career. It is intended to be used as a guide for people who understand the relationship of plain old-fashioned hard work and success in business, and as an inspiration for those who are simply unwilling to surrender their personal lives for that success. In real estate sales, success comes, to a great extent, from a willingness to do things that those content with ordinary production are *unwilling* to do. It is a commonly held belief in real estate that those who are producing at strong levels work all the time and have no personal life. This book is proof that this is a myth.

This book is not about the highest level of production possible, but about how one agent in a perfectly ordinary market place took advantage of every possible learning opportunity and created a business that produces a six-figure income, while ruthlessly protecting her personal time and achieving great satisfaction in balancing both.

Everybody starts somewhere. I will share with you briefly how I started and how, from a very humble beginning, my career evolved into a level of production I would not have thought possible in the early days.

When I started my real estate career in the spring of 1977, I lived in a very small town in the upper midwest, Vermillion, South Dakota, population: 10,000. We sold a ton of property despite the town's size, with a market fueled and primarily driven by the natural turnover at the University of South Dakota.

As an industry, our real estate community had no formal structure and was so unsophisticated that we didn't even have a Multiple Listing Service. We had no association, nor were we a part of any other formal real estate organization. We were not even so much as members of the National Association of Realtors.

Because of this, we had no opportunity for training and high quality education, and certainly no chance for mentoring. My early training was all 'in the trenches,' as they say, and there was nothing formal about it. It was a simple matter of following around and emulating the people I admired and paying attention to avoid the behaviors of people who appeared to be less successful than what I had in mind for my career.

Looking back, I realize that we were very fortunate to be doing business in a town where we had significant turnover in university personnel and equally fortunate that the town was so small that becoming well-known and recognized was fairly easy to do. In those days, and in that place, nobody thought consciously of personal promotion in the sense that marketing is done today. Nobody had any thought of spending any of their own money to place personal ads in the local paper, or to do a personal brochure, or any of the things that are recognized as essential elements of today's marketing campaigns.

I almost cringe now at the thought of the corny little newsletter I did - sent only to what I now know as my sphere of influence, but at the time, unfamiliar with the term, just to friends and others who would probably refer business to me if I just kept reminding them to do so. Probably the only redeeming qualities of that amateurish piece was that it was consistent, and that I was literally *the only agent in town* who was doing it.

I was able to build quickly and sustain for over ten years a pretty strong level of activity, even during the double-digit interest rates of the early to mid-eighties, simply by going around talking to people *all the time* about real estate. At the time, I was so broke I *had* to succeed, and in all honesty, it never occurred to me that maybe I wouldn't. At that time, I had no knowledge of the outrageously high failure rate industry-wide, and had no idea that although it's relatively easy to get into the real estate business, staying a long time and being successful is another matter entirely.

In that sense, I guess it was good that we were so isolated from the rest of the real estate world. Granted, we had no place to go for training and marketing ideas, but we also had nobody else's failures to discourage us.

When my husband, Brad, and I moved to Flagstaff, Arizona, in 1989, I remember vividly being awed by the difference in the real estate community here. I thought the Multiple Listing concept was the greatest thing since Paul Mitchell hairspray. Those people met every Thursday morning, associated with one another in a perfectly civilized manner, thanked one another publicly for selling their listings, responded favorably to other agents' requests for certain types of property, and on top of all *that they were computerized.*

I thought the Flagstaff real estate community was the most sophisticated organization in existence. After twelve years in this marketplace, I have long since come to realize that in truth, we are a pretty unpretentious, down-to-earth group that is still somewhat old-fashioned compared to other markets. We are, however, pretty well-organized, pretty well-connected to sources for just about any kind of training or marketing opportunity anyone could hope for, and we do have a *lot* of very good, dedicated, highly professional agents.

Since there is no licensing reciprocity from one state to another, I had to spend some time in real estate school, learning the market and the players. During that time, I had read about this guy named Mike Ferry, in California, who was mentoring people and guiding them to unbelievable heights in real estate production. I can't describe the excitement I felt in discovering that he would be the keynote speaker at the Arizona Association of Realtors Convention in August of '91.

I knew we didn't have money to attend the entire convention and stay at an expensive resort hotel, but I knew I *had to be there* for Mike's presentation. Until then, I'd spent a frustrating and unproductive year walking around the lake by our house in the evenings with my husband, crying and saying, *"I don't know what's wrong, but I can't do this any more,"* with him saying, *"Yes you can. You were a great agent before, just give it a chance."* I had spent that entire year setting Open Houses, taking a lot of floor time, and working a lot of hours, all the things that *appeared* to be the ingredients of success, and still very little had happened. Our personal resources had been drained because we came to Arizona to build our hotel, which my husband manages, and still, I had to find a way to get to Mike's presentation.

As always, when faced with a situation where we needed to figure out how to do the impossible, we walked around the lake discussing what I had read about this Mike Ferry guy and the incredible things he was teaching people to do. By the end of that hour, Brad had volunteered to drive me down to Phoenix, since at that time I was still intimidated by city traffic after Vermillion's 10,000 population. We'd go the night before so I could get up early and get a good seat; we'd stay at a nearby motel that wouldn't be as expensive as the convention resort, and we'd put it on a credit card because we truly had no cash to spare. To say that was the most important investment we've ever made in my career would be a *huge* understatement.

I sat in the center aisle seat in the second row, taking notes fast and furiously the whole time, and my life has literally never been the same since that day. Mike talked about a lot of things that seemed pretty revolutionary at the time. Today, eleven years later, many are standard procedure for strong productive agents.

He talked about getting a computer, hiring an assistant, canceling any scheduled Open Houses, telling our Brokers to take us off the floor time schedule, and getting *seriously* into an aggressive prospecting habit. I went home and did *all of that,* even as a newcomer to town with no business and no money. It took all the courage I've ever even *thought* of having, but I knew intuitively that Mike was right and this was my chance.

I would not have been able to take that leap of faith without Brad's steadfast support and constant encouragement, and his agreement to borrow money for me to launch this bold plan. I am truly grateful to him for believing in me, and to Mike Ferry for the great training that followed, and for the many extraordinary life lessons that have had such a profound affect on my career and on our life.

After several years of attending Mike's programs and learning the mindset of success, the techniques for effective prospecting, and the fundamentals of business planning, I had the good fortune of finding Lauren Harper-Haden, a very strong producer and the Queen of effective personal promotion through the use of a great newsletter, and Dave Beson who is the Master of great follow-up through his unparalleled multi-year, multi-occasion letter campaign, and David Knox, the Champion of right pricing. I also met Howard Brinton, the King of Team Building, who runs the country's greatest clearing house for proven personal marketing ideas from the best agents nationwide, and the best of the best in Canada.

I still attend their programs and learn the latest and greatest ideas, along with enjoying the opportunity to network one-on-one with the great agents who developed them. I do not pretend to be among the mega-producers who appear on panels with these great mentors. That's not my story. It's worth repeating that this book is about how one agent in a perfectly ordinary marketplace with no industry, started at zero and created a thriving business that continues to generate a solid six-figure income, while ruthlessly protecting my personal time, by always paying attention to learn from people who know more and do more than I do. You can do the same thing, and I sincerely hope this book will guide you to all the success you dream of, all the satisfaction you hope for, and to the balanced life you deserve. Have fun on the journey.

Section I:
Mental Preparation

Chapter One:
The Mindset Of Success

Goals, Dreams, Expectations

Think Big. Think *really* big. The more you put into your mind, the more you will achieve. Earl Nightengale taught us that man's problem is not in *achieving* his goal, but in ever having set the goal. Goal setting is a huge part of achievement, but before you even get to the goal setting stage, you have to spend some time on mindset and expectation.

A big part of this is spent in the dreaming stage. A goal is a dream with a deadline, so naturally you need to dream before you can establish a clear goal plan. This requires a lot of thought, and the more detailed and specific, the better. Most everyone would agree that it's better to have money than not to have it, but that doesn't tell us anything useful that can be a part of a goal plan, or assist us with expectation.

Mindset is an important part of the discussion on making a lot of money in *any* field. In real estate sales it definitely is, because for the most part, we're either going to succeed as *individuals* or we're not. Nobody else can do this for us. Much of this is determined by mindset: first of all, what's *a lot*? If we think $100,000 is a lot, we'll make $100,000. If we think $200,000 or $300,000 is a lot, that's exactly what we'll make. For people whose brass ring is a million dollars, two million, three million, that's exactly where they land. Given that we all get what we expect, let's establish that right now as a critical part of this entire process. Let's get very clear that we need to pay attention to what we expect since that's what we're going to get.

EXAMINING THE WHY

Ask yourself these important pre-goal setting questions:

- Why do I want to earn a six figure income?
- Why is this important?
- What will it do for me?
- How will it look and feel?

Regarding the actual formulation of goals, ask yourself:

- What is meaningful to me?
- What are my dreams?
- What would I do if there were no limits?
- What is my secret passion?

WRITING YOUR OWN LIFE SCRIPT

In the process of dreaming your way to a colorful, exciting life, don't hold back. This is your dream, and you can dream it any way you want. Think seriously and creatively about what you would do in life if there were no limits. Complete this statement:

If I could write the script for the story of my life, I would:

_____
_____
_____
_____
_____

Examining the Why

After completing this exercise, re-read your Life Script and ask yourself:

- Why do I want this?
- What will this do for me?
- How will it look and feel?
- What will it allow me to do?

Goal Planning Guide

Now use the Goal Planning Guide to help you go into greater detail.

- The house I live in will be:
- The furnishings and décor of my home will be:
- The car I drive will be:
- My investments will include:
- My clothes will be:
- My vacations will be:
- The hobbies I pursue will be:
- My toys will be:
- Spending time with family and friends will include:
- Entertainment and entertaining will include:
- Giving to others will include:
- Other secret passions will include:

> ### Everything Has a Price
>
> Everything has a price, so we need to examine what that price might be and how we're going to deal with it. Ask yourself:
>
> - Am I clear on the price I *personally* have to pay?
> - Am I truly committed to paying it?
> - What could stop me?
> - How will I resolve that?

We've established as fact that *everything has a price*, so let's not get in our goal plan anything for which we are not fully committed to paying the price. Our subject here is career success so obviously, the biggest price we have to be prepared to pay is the work effort. Without committing to the necessary work effort, the rest would all just be pie-in-the-sky pointless fantasy.

In committing to the necessary work effort, we need to internalize and practice success behaviors and daily habits. To do that, let's look at our present habits and ask ourselves these key questions:

> ### Ask Yourself
>
> - Does my work ethic match my dreams?
> - Am I accustomed to a dedicated work effort?
> - When I set my goal plan, will I really follow it?
> - Am I as committed as the work requires?

During the process of developing your goals, it's important to examine *everything* you need from your career success. The financial rewards are just one part of it, and usually not the singular motivator. At what level do you need the recognition?

Six Figure Income

Ask Yourself

Do you have a deep driving need to be:

- The Top Producer in your office?
- The Top Producer in your market?
- Ranked nationally in your franchise?
- The Top Producer nationally in your franchise?

What exactly will this level of success do for you? Will it bring you:

- The respect of your family and friends?
- The respect of your community?
- An ability to inspire others?
- Internal satisfaction from an exciting career?

Attitudes and Beliefs About Money

All of those are good reasons to do the things necessary to be successful. It's important to know yourself and know which of these needs is driving you and why they are important to you. These will become an important part of the mindset you carry with you on a daily basis and will help define the way you see yourself.

Before we can go into detail in putting our goal plan together, we need to examine how we feel about money. Many of us came from neighborhoods and families where having money was viewed as something that could only be achieved by the highest echelon of our society, and in the fifties and sixties Americana, that meant doctors and lawyers. We may even have grown up believing that it's not good to have money, and that if you acquire much, you'll become a ruthless tyrant.

I like Zig Ziglar's mantra that he believes the *"diamonds and gold are for God's people,"* or something very close to that thought. The rewards of success are not for bad people, Zig teaches, and I think he's right.

The Impact of Our Belief System

If you grew up with the Lake Woebegone mentality of Garrison Keillor's hysterically funny books about growing up in the ultra-conservative upper midwest, where if you had any more money than you *absolutely had to have* to pay your bills, you went to a lot of trouble to conceal your success, you've probably got some work to do. One of Mr. Keillor's best stories is about two older couples from Minnesota who were planning a trip to Hawaii years ago before that was a fairly common practice. One of the men didn't want anyone to know that he was just flat-out spending the obscene amount of money necessary for something so frivolous, and of course, everybody in town and everybody in the entire farm community knew about it. So he concocted an elaborate story about how his wife's sister and brother-in-law could get a better deal on *their* tickets if they could enlist a second couple to accompany them, and if he didn't consent to go, it would cause a catastrophic riff in his wife's family.

If you fear money and success to that extent, chances are pretty good that you'll go to a lot of trouble to make sure that doesn't become a problem.

In truth, most of us are probably amused by stories such as this and believe they don't apply to us, but the fact is, we need to speak to our pre-conditioning and self-doubt in this regard and put them away so we can move forward with the expectation of success. Now we need to examine our attitudes about money. We need to take a look at:

Ask Yourself

- How will changing income levels change my life?
- How will it change me?
- How will it affect my relationships?
- How do I feel about that?

Some of the things we need to include in our thought process are:

- So what if I grew up without money?
- How much do I really care about what the neighbors think?
- Anybody from any background can be successful.

Brian Tracy does a lot with resource material on the mindset of success. He has a great tape album that I'll bet I listened to a hundred times right after I got it, and of course, now it all fits. Internalizing that kind of information by repetitive listening and focus on the message is a great thing. Before I met Brian at one of Mike Ferry's retreats and got my own set of his tapes, I borrowed his *Success Secrets Of Self-Made Millionaires* from a friend and kept it in my car, listening to it daily for over six months. When you're heavily in debt and driving an old car, you have to concentrate on the mindset it takes to achieve success.

The two most important factors in the success formula, without a doubt, are *work effort* and *mindset*. You can work your butt off and unless you believe passionately, and can actually *see yourself successful*, you'll just be busy with no money. Conversely, if you have the dream, the vision, the desire, and won't commit to the work ethic required to get there, you'll just be a dreamer.

The two truly do go hand-in-hand. Throughout this book, I'll tell you a lot about the work effort, but for extensive exploration of mindset, I'm going to refer you to Brian Tracy and Mark Victor Hansen. Both talk a lot about visualization, and although Mark is best known for his phenomenally successful *Chicken Soup For The Soul* books co-authored with Jack Canfield, he's done some great stuff in the area of career success.

Mark advocates the use of a technique called 'Treasure Mapping.' That's a process of cutting out photos and pictures from magazines, catalogs, travel brochures, car dealership brochures, house plan books, etc. and pasting them on a poster board where you can see them every day. This is done after you've set your goals for the year, and the treasure map is used as a visual reminder of what you've put in your goal plan.

I've been doing this for years and I generally add great phrases, also clipped from magazines and brochures, of things that are important in my goal plan. I also like to add a check for the amount of money I plan to earn that year. This is a fun exercise, and it can be enormously helpful in keeping your eye on the prize, so to speak, as a constant reminder of the why.

I keep my treasure map hanging inside my closet door at home because there are some parts of it, such as the check made out to me and dated the last day of the year, and some other personal things that for me, are a little too private to display anywhere else. I do, however, have several friends whose treasure maps grace the walls of their offices, where they'll be able to see them all day, every day as reminders of why they do what they do.

I personally think it's fun to do treasure mapping in a group of like-minded colleagues. I learned about it from one of my early Flagstaff brokers who had attended one of Mark's seminars and brought this valuable idea back to share with us. Since that first time, I've done it annually with other groups, always well-attended, and everyone seemed to value the exercise and hung onto their maps. Only once did I ever hear someone involved in the exercise say she wasn't sure exactly how it worked, but that stuff just magically appeared in her life. Forget that. This is a simple principle of getting what you *expect* based on the work effort you're willing to put forth.

That's why it's critical to have goals that are written, reviewed often, and upgraded or adjusted as necessary. In my view, it's also important to have the visualization before you on a regular basis, showing what success looks like to you, and therefore, to be able to invoke *how it feels* when you need it most.

I see my treasure map every time I change clothes or otherwise open my closet, so that's a minimum of twice a day, and usually more often than that. You'll know if you feel it'll be better for you to have yours at your office. That's a personal decision, but the key to focus on is that daily reminders reinforce your beliefs about what you can do.

Another thing I've done is to make a mini-treasure map and tuck it inside the front of my Day Timer. In much the same manner that it's really helpful to review your affirmations daily, which we will discuss shortly, I really think it's good to also keep the tangible visualization in constant view. I like the mini-treasure map for short term goals, such as an extra special outfit for a big occasion. When I look at it, I'm aware that I will buy it only *when* I have achieved the goals it represents: I need to be at a specified level of production, and at a certain weight and size. I am a person who is and always has been enormously grateful for my opportunities, which is why I almost always tie the things that I think are a big deal opportunity to a reward for having *done* something else. Here's an example:

I was so awed by my first attendance of Mike Ferry's annual Superstar Retreat, that I spent an entire year leading up to it. When I first heard him speak at the Arizona Convention in August of '91, he had just held that year's retreat, so I was going to have to wait clear until the following August. From that first time in 1992, it was an annual ritual that I would register for the retreat and reserve my hotel room on January second. I made a huge deal out of it. Those two calls were scheduled in my Day Timer months in advance, and when the confirmation slips came in the mail, I put them on my treasure map. Those things reminded me of my good fortune in having the opportunity to attend the retreat, and that I'd better keep working pretty diligently. The trip, the conference, and the new clothes were going to be a sizeable investment. Naturally, it would be irresponsible to neglect any of the basics to do this, so it kept me focused on the importance of a strong, consistent work effort, so I could be sure the money would be there.

SEE YOURSELF SUCCESSFUL

This is a tremendously important part of internalizing the mindset of success, and it's only one of a handful of activities you really need to incorporate into your daily routine. With the work effort and belief system of success and full expectation of high achievement, there are *literally no limits* to what we can accomplish.

Over time, these activities will become as natural to you as breathing, but for now, just start with your big treasure map (for the entire year, or more than one year), a mini-treasure map that you carry with you all the time (for short-term goals), half a dozen or so affirmations, and tapes by the legendary experts that focus on mindset and expectations. These things are critical for anybody who wants to achieve success and maintain it, but they are particularly vital to anyone who is the first person ever in the history of their family to achieve this kind of success.

Let's review how to make your own treasure map. As we've discussed here, put a lot of stuff on it; give this a lot of thought and really get into it. *Don't be bashful.* Somebody once told me that if nobody laughs when you state your goals, they aren't high enough. Isn't that a great thought? It's your treasure map, so do it your way and use it to help lead you to your definition of the success you want. Remember this is the visual reminder that will help you stay focused, and will be tremendously helpful once you've taken your written goals and put them in the form of a business plan.

> **MAKE A TREASURE MAP**
>
> To make your treasure map, you'll need:
>
> - Poster board
> - Glue sticks
> - Scissors
> - Magazines
> - Travel brochures
> - Car dealership brochures
> - House plan books
> - Hobby related brochures

The more detailed you can make your treasure map, the better. The same is true of your written goals and ultimately of your business plan.

The business plan is the thing that takes your overall goal plan and breaks it down into the individual activities that need to be done to achieve the goals, and finally down into the tiniest steps within each activity. This is crucial to high achievement, and if you've never written a business plan, it's an exercise I know you'll enjoy learning to do, and you'll feel great about cultivating the habit of *working* from a business plan. We'll spend more time on that later, but for now I just mention it in the context of the mindset of success because it's an important tool that will help you in that regard.

Another tool that will help you cultivate the mindset you need to break into the six-figure earnings category for the first time, then ultimately to stay there and increase as a matter of habit, is affirmations. These are positive statements made from the perspective of having already accomplished your goals. The subconscious mind accepts as truth whatever we tell it, which is why it's critical to use positive success-affirming statements to combat the doubt and fear-induced negatives.

Here's an example: *"I confidently complete an hour of phone prospecting every morning, securing enough listing appointments to earn $160,000 this year."*

Another good one that's much shorter is: *"I'm GOOD on the phone."*

Give a lot of thought to the ideas you want implanted in your mind to help propel you to the achievement of your goals.

When you've decided what you want as affirmations, write them out exactly as you want to review them and internalize them; they can be upgraded as needed, but for now, start with at least six, maybe as many as a dozen.

Affirmations

Some ideas to help you get started are:

- I enjoy working five highly productive days per week.
- I feel good about getting to my office at 7:00 A.M.
- I always work diligently to make my time highly productive.
- My prospecting results in a lot of appointments, not just 'leads.'
- I take right-priced listings everyday.

When you've completed the process of writing out your affirmations, record them in your own voice and listen to that tape on your way to work every day for at least the next two months. You'll probably find this tool to be so powerful that you'll want to continue it always but I suggest two months, because you may want to make a new tape at that time, with the expectation of continuing this great habit.

How about this affirmation: *"I surround myself with positive people who are committed to excellence."* Now this one carries some other implications because it's the first of our affirmations that involves anybody else. Re-read this section and you'll see that until we arrived at this thought, we affirmed only our own behaviors; things we can control. We cannot control the behaviors and attitudes of others, but we don't have to accept them. It's critical that we stay away from the nay-sayers, which is anybody who is going to rain on our parade and put us at risk of buying into any of the self-doubt that becomes *their* excuse for not accomplishing anything.

At work it's fairly easy to stay away from the nay-sayers. Usually they're the people who just sit in the office waiting for something to fall into their laps, even though their past experiences tell them that's not likely. When that self-fulfilling prophecy comes true, they've gotten exactly what they expected, so they're adding to their bank of negative experience. They probably think they're doing you a favor by warning you not to get your hopes up. RUN. Get away from that kind of thinking as quickly as possible.

You can do this pretty easily by just closing your door if you have one, or by excusing yourself from the conversation and picking up the phone if you don't have a private office. Nobody wants to get the reputation as the office 'hot dog' by just coming right out and saying, *"Get away from me, you're contaminating my thoughts."* There are much classier ways to do this, and if you always do it pleasantly, they'll eventually get the hint and find another audience. A great agent whom I admire immensely had a chain that stretched all the way across her open cubicle to let everyone know that her 'door' was closed because her work at that moment was important and not open to interruption. I never once heard her tell anybody to stop disturbing her in the entire five years we worked together. When the chain was in place, it spoke for itself and the message was abundantly clear.

You are under no obligation to accept every invitation to a negative conversation. If you have to deal with this at home, it's quite another matter, I will repeat, however, stay away from the nay-sayers. . . *all of them*. If you have any negativism at home, try the *"I really need your help"* approach. Explain that what you're doing precludes any negativity and you'd really appreciate their help in keeping it away from you.

I've never had to deal with this on a first-tier relationship level, because that's not how we do things at our house. Whenever I go to a great conference and learn something new I want to incorporate into my business, I always brain-storm it with Brad, and half the time he's the one trying to figure out how we can pay for implementing it.

Our sons, Pat and Tim, are grown and away from home, but we talk often and always know what's going on in each other's lives, and both of them are enormously supportive. From them I get comments like *"You're amazing."* and *"You go girl."*

This is actually the Napoleon Hill concept of 'Master Minding,' which we'll discuss in depth in the next chapter. In its simplest form, Napoleon Hill taught that two (or more) people brain-storming any concept or idea will always come up with far more positive ways to take action and implement the idea into reality than one person acting alone. We've always done that and we've always believed that both of us have accomplished much more than we would have alone, because we've had such a strong Master Mind alliance with each other.

Chapter Two:
Master-Minding

The Master Mind Alliance

If you don't have this connection, or if you have negativism in any fashion from the second tier of your relationships: your parents, in-laws, siblings, you will definitely need a Master Mind Group. You obviously won't want to terminate your relationships with these folks, but you may need to limit the amount of time you spend with them, or you may need to establish some ground rules. Think of it as enlisting their support, and realize that it's critical to be immersed in the positives in every way possible.

You may want to just come right out and tell them you're involved in a huge undertaking that is very important to you, and you just can't risk being sidetracked by any negativity. If some of the people in your life are *extremely negative,* they're probably also a little dense about it and you may have to take a slightly different approach. Everybody *loves* to be asked for their help; it makes us all feel important and valued. You may do better with a parent or sibling if you tell them about this big undertaking, and tell them that as one of the most important people in your life, you're really counting on their help in keeping negatives away and surrounding yourself with positives. If they pay attention and react favorably, you'll be doing *them* a huge favor in helping them rid themselves of some of their own negativism.

Another part of staying away from nay-sayers and surrounding yourself with positive thinkers is by attending programs, The negative folks do not go to conferences, seminars, retreats, or training events. They're so busy doing what they've always done, which is mostly sitting there waiting for something to happen, that they can't be going to any of the really good trainers to learn anything. Only positive thinkers who want to do better will attend. So just by going, you'll be surrounded for the entire program by people who are just like you: those who are constantly looking to improve.

I recommend doing this a minimum of every six months, and if you can possibly do it, quarterly is even better. You'll find that people share very freely when they're not in their own marketplace. Nobody cares if you copy them, we just all want to be careful not to tell our biggest competitor our best secret of success. So go someplace that's a fairly good distance away, and you're almost sure you'll never run into anyone you know. In nearly twelve years of attending great programs on a national level, I have yet to run into anyone from my own town, *ever*. There are several great agents in our MLS, so I have to believe they're getting their training and great ideas somewhere other than the programs I attend. Don't overlook your company's annual national or international convention. The speakers at these will be very high quality, and so will the attendees.

Two things you can do as spin offs from attending great educational events are:

- Get the tapes of the program itself, or those by one or more of the main speakers and listen to them frequently and systematically. Listening to each tape in a cassette album for fourteen days before you move on to the next one is a great way to really get to know the material, internalize it, and incorporate it into your business.

- Get involved in a Master Mind Group of other attendees. If you're on the lookout, you may find some good agents who live a couple of hours' driving time away from your marketplace, so they'll be willing to share ideas freely and it'll still be workable for you to get together on a regular basis.

THE POWER OF TWO... OR MORE

I was in a very effective Master Mind Group with some people from various areas of Phoenix and Tucson for several years. On the first Friday of each month we all met in Phoenix, which was the central point for all of us, for dinner and two or three hours of lively discussion.

MASTER MIND GROUP DISCUSSIONS

Each month we talked about:

- What was working well
- Everybody's latest and greatest ideas (with copies for everybody)
- The best things we were all reading
- What we needed help with

It was great. I once got worried because I had my phone scripts down pat, and was pretty disciplined about my prospecting time, but I wasn't getting the results I needed regarding the number of appointments being scheduled. Without hesitation, one of my friends said, *"Why aren't you calling FSBOs and Expireds?"* And there it was. He was absolutely right, and I'd been too close to see it, for whatever reason. These are two groups of prospects with a *known real estate need,* and if you know what to say and you're making your calls, there's no way you wouldn't be getting the appointments.

We all helped each other with things like that and everybody improved. One of our members was taking a lot of referral business until we brain-stormed it and she realized she was actually *losing* money on each one because of the way she had expenses and staff compensation set up. Together we were able to figure out a way she could make a couple of adjustments and end up profitable.

Another thing we did every time we met, each of us brought the most important thing we'd learned from any source since our last time together, again with enough copies to share with everyone. Sometimes we'd come away with a great ad idea, sometimes a killer pre-listing package, sometimes a really unique customer service idea. It was wonderfully resourceful.

We also combined everybody who was anybody's recommended reading list, from Oprah to Mike Ferry. Then we'd each read a book from the list and present sort of an old-fashioned book report, along with a recommendation of whether it was the type of book where you could get the main ideas this way, or if it was the type of thing where it really should be read in its entirety.

Those meetings were a great way to stay in touch with a terrific group of people with a similar vision, and to know that each time we'd find complete acceptance from the real-life viewpoint of those who were out there every day, up against the same challenges in a highly competitive industry.

Our group once went so far as to have a weekend retreat at a member's cabin in the White Mountains. One of the best things we did there was to video tape everybody's listing presentation. What a great learning experience. We all role-played, so everybody helped one another, and we all learned from each other, but nothing was stronger than what we learned from ourselves and about ourselves. I highly recommend doing this. Over the years, my family and friends have been great about helping me with role-playing situations, but nothing is more effective than doing this with your Master Mind Group. Everybody there is good, and you all know it, so it helps you really make the effort required to be very sharp. Also, those who are playing the role of the prospect have the experience to interject true-to-life responses, questions, and comments that actually do come up every day. Seeing yourself on video tape is truly an exercise in brutal honesty. It's incredibly effective.

The ideal size for a Master Mind Group is about ten. Our group started with eight, we added a couple more members later, and we found that size to be very workable. It becomes a different type of event if the group is larger. Then you have to start concerning yourself with places that can accommodate the group, and in my humble but correct opinion, you spend more time on logistics than content.

A group of ten can usually fit at almost any restaurant and in most anyone's home. A mixture of both types of meetings is nice over the course of a year. We found several places in Phoenix that were very happy to have our business, understood the need for separate checks with receipts, and always made the extra effort to seat us where we could talk. Nobody ever minded our being there two to three hours, and they always welcomed us back. We tried to go out of our way to be courteous and accurate with our reservation count, we were always appreciative, and we always made sure we were generous tippers.

Another thing a Master Mind Group offers is the trusted friends you may need between meetings. If you have a situation that can't wait until your next regularly scheduled meeting, and needs to be brain-stormed with somebody who is probably in the best position to have a solution, you'll know from the time you've spent together who is the best person to call. It's amazing how often someone in your group will have faced the exact same situation, or something so similar that together you can see an obvious solution. The best of all worlds, of course, is an obvious and *simple* solution, and quite often you'll find that.

Surrounding Yourself With Productivity

It's very important that you spend some time with people who are doing more than you're doing. That's another compelling reason to go to programs on a national level and to be a strong participant in a Master Mind Group. Chances are you're the Top Producer in your office, and you're probably among the Top Producers in your marketplace. To keep growing, you need constant exposure to new ideas, techniques, marketing strategies that are working, the opportunity to learn *why* they're working, and how you can make them work for you. And when it's time to raise the bar, you need some solid anchors in your belief system that you can do it. That will best come from having seen somebody else that's done it. In my opinion, there's a big difference between *reading* about somebody who's done it, and *seeing, meeting, and hearing*.

- Seeing that they're a regular person just like you

- Meeting them in person and talking to them

- Hearing their story and *precisely* how they did it

It has always amazed me that, invariably, the bigger and better a person's production is, the more open and willing to share they always are. Chances are good that in the course of conversation, they'll tell you something indicating that they know you can do it, too. Write that down and put it on your treasure map and in your affirmations. It'll help you to be reminded often that someone you admire sees the promise of success in you.

Obviously, the national events are great for camaraderie, friendships, and in our particular business, for referrals. Many of the best referrals I get and send out are from friends I see once or twice a year at the big national events. I have several friendships that go all the way back to the first big event I attended in 1992, and we always look forward to reconnecting. Typically, I'll get half a dozen or so calls and emails the last week before flying out to attend a conference. Almost always, it's friends wanting to make sure we have dinner together, or maybe breakfast, or go to an attraction such as Graceland if we're in Memphis, Disney World when we're in Orlando, etc. Most of the time you can count on it that they'll bring somebody else along, or maybe you'll want to, and you'll end up in a lively discussion with a fun and interesting group of people. That is Master Minding at its very best.

I have a rule that whenever I'm at a conference, each day I sit next to someone I don't know, and I always ask each one, *"What's the best thing you've learned at this conference?"* Quite often you'll hear an idea that will either answer a question you've had in your mind, or you'll discover a particularly good break-out session you'll want to attend. Sometimes it'll give you a new spin on something you've been wanting to try, but it just didn't quite fit in the form you knew about before. The great thing about conferences is that if you're looking, you *will* find somebody with an answer to your question, or someone who can help you bring together a plan for a new idea.

> ### Straight From The Masters
>
> Obviously, the resource books, trade journals, and the internet are great for information, but at a conference you can talk directly to:
>
> - A presenter.
> - A speaker.
> - A panelist.
> - Another agent.
>
> You can ask them:
>
> - *"After you did this and said that, **then what**?"*
> - *"How did you handle this?"*
> - *"What would you do if the prospect said this?"*

In my experience, the speakers, presenters, and panelists are incredibly generous with their time and very kind about offering suggestions and solutions, Interestingly, they are also always amazingly approachable.

Creating Your Own Master Mind Group

Sometimes, in the proper context and if the circumstances are right, they may even agree to a one-on-one meeting by accepting your invitation to breakfast or lunch. You'll probably want to get several other people together, so others can benefit from their experience and advice as well. Several years ago, our entire Master Mind Group had the good fortune of having lunch with one of the panelists at a major national conference. This was possible because she was a personal friend of one of our members, and rather than keep her all to themselves, they invited all the rest of us. What a treat. We had a group of about twelve or fourteen people, and she was so gracious and generous in her sharing of ideas and practical advice. Another fine example of Master Minding.

Always remember to send your thank you notes. I like to keep a running list in front of my writing portfolio and add to it each day of the conference, the name of anybody who has gone out of their way to share and be helpful. Tuck their card right behind the list and when you get back to your hotel room, put that day's cards in an envelope marked 'Thank You Notes.' Then when you get home they're all together and handy along with the list, which you've added to the envelope at the end of the conference.

Everybody loves nice personal handwritten notes, and nobody's doing them any more. They are a *great* way to be remembered. The next year when you're ready to attend the same conference, you'll not only be invited to the special lunches and dinners again, people will tell you how much they loved your note and what a pleasant surprise it was. I actually do it just because it's *always* good manners to say *"thank you,"* but as an unexpected bonus, I've ended up with some great new friends.

SECTION II:
THE FOUNDATION OF YOUR BUSINESS

Chapter Three:
Working From A Business Plan

Treat it Like a Business

It's interesting that the highest level of success is always achieved by the agents who have a detailed plan, a road map of sorts, and who have the ability to remain focused. Most agents do not have a formal plan.

Real Estate is a very detail-oriented business, and most of the details are so important that without a plan, it's easy to get so absorbed in them that the steps leading toward high volume production just don't ever fit in.

This needs to be turned completely around, with the focus on the production, and the details put into duplicatable systems, delegated to others. We also need to establish the mindset that we are going to treat our sales career like a business.

Business Systems

A sales career that is treated like a business, rather than a job, incorporates the daily use of systems that are:

- Measurable
- Duplicatable
- Predictable

My goal for you is to make your plan and your business *work for you* in such a way that it does not eclipse your life. You will hear me say repeatedly that work is not life; it is what we do to *fund* life. The best way, in my opinion, to maintain this perspective is to work from a business plan, which is the foundation for your business.

In writing your business plan, begin at the end. Begin with your income goal, then divide by your average commission and you will know the number of transactions you need to close. From there, you can break the plan down to the number of listings, appointments, leads, contacts, calls attempted, and finally to the number of hours you need to spend prospecting.

BEGIN AT THE END / EXAMPLE 1

Income Goal — $160,000

Average Commission — $5,250

Transactions Closed — 31

Listings (2/1 ratio = 31 x 2) — 62

Appointments (2/1 ratio = 62 x 2) — 124

Leads (4/1 ratio = 124 x 4) — 496

Contacts (5/1 ratio = 496 x 5) — 2,480

Attempts (4/1 ratio = 2,480 x 4) — 9,920

Attempts/Hour (15) (9,920/15) — 661.33 Hr.

Days Worked/Year (250) (661.33/250) Daily prospecting — 2.65 Hr.

You can see from this example that the following assumptions are made:

➢ One of every two listings becomes a closed transaction.

➢ One of every two appointments results in a listing.

➢ One of every four leads schedules an appointment.

➢ One of every five contacts becomes a lead.

➢ One of every four call attempts results in a contact.

➢ Fifteen attempts can be completed in an hour.

➢ Five work days times fifty weeks allows two weeks vacation.

Six Figure Income

Some of these numbers are somewhat optimistic, but this exercise also assumes that you are *not making cold calls*. In the next chapter I will explain how you can get into a serious prospecting habit without cold calls.

Some of the other numbers in this example are on the conservative side, and there are several things you can do to influence them in your favor. You can see by looking at the sample business plan, that if you practice your listing presentation and get very good at it, you will take the listing more than 50% of the time. If you practice your prospecting scripts and dialogs *and* call a lot of *high impact* prospects (those with a known real estate need) you can dramatically affect the number of leads and appointments that will result.

The Numbers

Use this formula for sixty to ninety days and keep track of your own numbers. I think you will find that you can actually *complete* fifteen (or maybe up to eighteen) conversations in an hour, rather than just that number of attempts. If that proves to be the case, the number of hours needed for daily prospecting could be substantially reduced.

For now, however, probably the most important thing you've learned from this exercise is that to make the projected income goal, 2.65 hours, or more realistically two and a half hours of prospecting will be necessary on a daily basis, if indeed, you have no repeat or referral business. This particular exercise also assumes that you take no Buyers during the year of this business plan. Let's see what happens by changing those two things:

Begin At The End / Example 2

Income Goal	$160,000
Average Commission	$5,250
# Transactions Closed	31
# Buyer Closings	5
# Repeat & Referral Closings	5
# Listings Closed	21
# Listings (2/1 ratio = 21 x 2)	42
# Appointments (2/1 ratio = 42 x 2)	84
# Leads (4/1 ratio = 84 x 4)	336
# Contacts (5/1 ratio = 336 x 5)	1,680
# Attempts (4/1 ratio = 1,680 x 4)	6,720
# Attempts/Hour (15) (6,720/15)	488 Hours
# Days Worked/Year (250) (488/250) Daily prospecting	1.79 Hr./Day

With those adjustments, we just moved the prospecting time from roughly two and one half hours daily to one and three quarters. Again, some of these ratios are probably conservative. As your business builds and you become more proficient, you will see many favorable adjustments that will be automatic.

Don't Over-Complicate

Thirty-one transactions, by today's standards, is not that big a deal and just not that tough to do. I wanted to make this exercise very simple so that people who are trying to break into the six-figure earnings bracket for the first time would be able to identify with it easily. You may decide you want to do fifty or sixty, which will result in a very nice income without disrupting your life to the point of no longer being worth it.

> **MANAGING SIXTY TRANSACTIONS**
>
> You can comfortably manage up to sixty transactions with just:
>
> ➤ One assistant
>
> ➤ Some out-sourcing
>
> ➤ Very good systems in place
>
> ➤ Carefully managed scheduling

The one number in these exercises that is not at all conservative is the average commission figure of $5,250. Unless you're already a 100% agent, you probably noticed that this is a very high figure. This is probably as good a time as any to say that I really believe all serious career agents in the six-figure income category should be where they can earn 100% commissions. On a split, you'd have to work your tail off to make the projected income goal, and it would require a lot more than thirty-one transactions. This is not a recruiting book, nor is it an endorsement for any particular franchise. There are a lot of great real estate franchises, some historically founded on the 100% concept, others based on a traditional commission split. Both have their place and both work very well for many people at various stages in their careers.

A couple of other things that need to be discussed in conjunction with a business plan are centered around the relationship of income to expenses. Your biggest dollar expense, as opposed to time expense, will obviously be personal promotion. In the early stages, you'll spend more as a percentage than you will later as your production increases.

Obviously, you want to put your name on everything appropriate, along with your company's logo. You are after all, promoting *yourself* so you can build *your business,* not somebody else's brokerage. Anything you pay for should have your name on it. Anything that has only the brokerage name, or that emphasizes the brokerage name, should be paid for by your Broker. Period. It's really that simple.

If you're on a commission split, you need to watch your contribution to the brokerage all the time, so you know when you need to take the necessary steps to make an adjustment. This will happen when you know you've contributed enough to be fair, but you may be paying too much. I'm not necessarily telling you to move to a 100% House, unless there's a really good one in your town, where you think you'd rather be. Do your homework first, so you know what your counterparts in the 100% offices are paying in monthly desk fees and office costs. Compare that with the percentage of your commission that goes to your Broker, and know what the brokerage provides for you and what that value amounts to. Then talk to your Broker about paying a monthly fee in exchange for retaining 100% of your commissions. Have several scenarios worked out so you *know* you're offering to pay your fair share, but no more than what's fair.

Whatever you do, *don't* become your own Broker. If you are a great salesperson, don't get into management. It *will* affect your production, and may even kill it. Unless you *truly* have a desire to be in management - to the extent that doing so showed up prominently in your goal setting session-and unless you live in a big enough market place where you can make great money on other people's production, don't do it. Pay your fair share, appreciate what your Broker provides for you, and use your time and resources to remain a great agent.

Chapter Four:
The 'P' Word: Prospecting

Telling the Whole World

The single biggest expense you'll ever have as an agent is the money you lose by not prospecting. There are many different ways to prospect, but the fact is, if you don't tell a lot of people every day what you sell and how well you sell it, you just won't sell much.

Conversely, telling a lot of people will result in a lot of sales. A marketing plan for a full year at a time, which incorporates all of the things you'll do that year to tell a lot of people what a great agent you are is crucial, and will be discussed in depth later, but sooner or later, you have to pick up the phone.

When we first moved to Arizona, my first concern was getting my numbers up as fast as I could, and with no money for an extensive marketing campaign, the telephone was the way to do that.

Do as much as you can stand, and do it early in the day. It's the toughest thing we have to do, but it's also the thing that is the most critical to our production. There are several reasons to do it first thing in the morning, but the biggest is that a lot of things will keep coming up throughout the day to prevent it, and if you don't prospect, you will not build a business. Period.

Prospecting is so important that we need to get in the habit of building our entire day around it, rather than putting ourselves at risk of having it get lost in the shuffle of a busy day and never getting around to it.

Later, after you've been at it awhile and have made some money, you'll be able to spend some of it on marketing and make your daily routine easier. The success of my newsletter, which we'll discuss at length in the section on personal marketing, a presence of over eleven years in this marketplace with repeat and referral business, and increased name recognition have all made it possible to reduce the amount of phone prospecting from what I did in the early stages. That's the way it works. Getting started as a new agent or jump-starting your career as an experienced agent, it's important to make the commitment of daily prospecting.

Confidence = Knowing What to Say

The single biggest reason people don't prospect is that they don't know what to say. They're afraid they'll come off sounding unprepared and therefore looking foolish. My business partner and I met at our office every morning for over a year and practiced our phone scripts, out loud, standing up (which the experts agree projects the greatest strength), and we're pretty good on the phone now. We know what to say, and it's as normal-sounding and natural as any conversation we'd have with a friend.

Don't worry about anybody laughing at you when you do this. Even if they do, they'll admire your commitment to succeed, and nobody ever laughs at the top producer. Never fall into the trap of thinking you're too cool to practice. All great agents practice sometime.

I'm not real big on pure 'cold calling.' In my mind, that's just calling people at random, without knowing if they even *own* their home, much less want to *sell* it. Call people with a known real estate need first: FSBOs and Expireds. If your market is strong, you may not have many expired listings, but call those you do have, and call every For-Sale-By-Owner every day and just keep asking them if they're ready to list with you. In your first call, the most important thing you want to know is motivation; so ask these two critical questions:

- *"Where are you moving?"*

- *"When do you need to be there?"*

After you've completed these calls, go to your 'Just Listed' and 'Just Sold' groups. Those are the neighbors around any property that has just been listed:

- To ask if they have any friends who have expressed an interest in the area.

It also includes the neighbors around a recent sale, especially if it's a popular area and the listing sold quickly. The piece of information you're looking for here is:

- When those neighbors are planning their next move.

If it's six months or less, get them in your contact management program and stay in touch regularly, offering information on property values, interest rates, home inspectors, etc.

Keep in mind, don't just prospect for leads, prospect for *appointments*. The first two groups, the FSBOs and Expireds will get you *right now* business. The other two will generate *future* business.

The next important group of calls is *anybody you know - everybody* you know that you could comfortably and ask:

- *"Who do you know that's planning on moving?"*

Reflexively, they'll almost all say *"I can't think of anybody,"* so you'll have to prompt them a little bit. Howard Brinton calls this *"going three deep,"* meaning you ask three times, (for an answer to any question) before you accept the original answer.

> ### Go Three Deep
>
> In this case, you'd go three deep by asking:
>
> ➤ *"What about anybody at work?"*
>
> ➤ *"How about your golf league?"*
>
> ➤ *"Is your company hiring?"*

Ask them if they mind if you check in with them from time to time. One of my friends is a master at this, and people call him all the time now with leads, after getting his reminder calls for over seven years that I know of. Now when anyone in his groups hears *anything* about somebody who wants to move, he's their man.

Your Million Dollar ABCs

Develop an ABC list of people you know and do your personal business with; this is your accountant, your beauty shop, car repair guy, dentist, etc. If you do business with them, you have every right to ask them to do business with you. Candidly, many of the people on your list will be entrepreneurs, too, and they'll catch on real fast that when you ask them for referrals, you'll probably be just as willing to *send them* referrals, and I guarantee you, after you train them to expect your calls, you will get some leads from them.

An hour a day of making this type of prospecting calls faithfully, consistently, will get you a lot of business. Two hours is better, if you can stand it. Now remember, these are not cold calls, so don't be intimidated, and don't be tempted to shy away from it until you give it an honest try. The really big guns do three, even four hours daily, and some even claim five or six. Frankly, I've never believed many people have the stomach for that. I've also wondered, when would they go on all the listing appointments they must be getting?

Another thing, a lot of people I've met over the years have tried to *hire* somebody to do their telephone prospecting. That is Bullshit Myth #1. Prospecting is the single factor that separates the great agent from the ordinary, and I *promise* you, if anybody has what it takes to stick with prospecting, they will do it for *themselves,* not for somebody else. Decide early that you're going to learn to do it right, practice diligently, get good at it, and stick with it. If you do *just that,* you will make a lot of money.

Your attitude toward prospecting needs to be that you're good at it, and that you get lots of revenue-generating appointments by doing it. Good prospecting habits will solve 95% of your problems. Always stay focused on that, and you'll be able to develop the great habit of prospecting daily. Howard Brinton calls it your 'Hour of Power,' and only you can decide as your business grows and develops if that hour should be sixty minutes, or maybe ninety, or maybe even a hundred and twenty.

It's worth repeating: work your entire day around your Hour of Power. Don't try to fit it in somewhere, or it won't get done. I actually recommend thirty minutes of script practice, followed immediately by your prospecting time. That will get you warmed up and ready to operate at peak efficiency. Have fifty-minute hours, with ten-minute breaks if you're doing multiple hours, Do not make or return any other calls until your prospecting time has been fully completed.

If there's an urgent call, instruct your assistant to call the client back and tell them when you'll return their call. I've always had my assistant tell callers I'm in an appointment, and the approximate time I'll be getting back to them. I've always been comfortable doing this because prospecting is an appointment, and it's right in my scheduler at the same time every day. Treat prospecting as a *sacred appointment* that cannot be broken any more than you'd break an appointment with a client, and you'll always have plenty of business.

Lesson From The Masters

My friend 'Dan' tells a great story from years ago when he was a rookie here in Flagstaff. He mentioned to his Broker, 'Mr. Douglas' that he wished he could be like 'Bob,' a highly successful agent whom he greatly admired. Bob always seemed to have all the business he could handle, and yet he played golf every day. Mr. Douglas said *"Oh, you can be. Let me show you how Bob does it."* Elated at the opportunity to learn the magic secret from the master, Dan followed Mr. Douglas through the building to Bob's office. Upon seeing the door closed, Dan was disappointed, thinking he wouldn't learn the secret after all, until Mr. Douglas said *"Lean against the door and listen carefully."* Feeling somewhat silly about doing this, he heard Bob talking in an excited, animated manner. Dan said to Mr. Douglas, *"Oh, he's got somebody in there with him,"* to which Mr. Douglas responded, *"He's got **everybody he knows** in there with him."* *"What do you mean,"* asked a very curious Dan. The older gentleman replied, *"He's on the phone, calling everybody he knows, asking them if they want to buy or sell anything: home, second home, investment property, land, **anything**. And he does that for at least an hour every day."* Dan believes this was probably the most important real estate training he's ever had.

Dan went over to RE/MAX a year before I did, and after I came in, I noticed he started asking me a lot of questions about this Mike Ferry guy I followed. It was common knowledge in the real estate community that I went to California two or three times a year by then, to learn more. It was from one of these conversations that we decided to commit to daily script practice and role-playing.

I'd been to a few of Mike's annual Superstar Retreats by then, as well as a 'Productivity School,' which is an excellent week-long program devoted entirely to scripts: phone-prospecting scripts, door-knocking scripts, listing presentation scripts, etc. I was also already in Mike's Business Planning Program, a process of adding accountability, which in my opinion is

Six Figure Income

often the missing element. In real estate we can look, act, be, and feel busy all the time and still not be making any money. The accountability factor is the assurance that you're going to stay on track by doing things the right way. I encouraged Dan to join Business Planning, which I explained would include being called each week at a specified time, and being asked very specific questions, and being expected to report certain numbers that had to be recorded daily regarding the results of prospecting. This would include number of calls made, number of appointments scheduled, number of listings taken, number of sales made, etc.

Practice Makes Perfect

That's when we started our daily script practice, and as mentioned earlier, we continued for over a year. We both felt this was the best daily exercise we ever did, and of course now we practice daily with live prospects and both of our production reflects that.

I highly recommend teaming up with somebody in your office to do this. I don't mean team up in the sense of a production team like so many of the mega producers are doing. I just mean find a script buddy and commit, and I can assure you, your production will improve. Look around for somebody who has a similar work ethic and production level as yours and approach them.

When Dan and I did this, we both moved into the six figure income category and we've stayed there. Show your friend this section of this book, and tell them this was done in a perfectly ordinary 50,000 population town with no industry and no dramatic influx of people driving the market. This is regular people, doing business in a regular town, with regular market conditions, but *tenaciously committed* to a somewhat irregular daily activity.

I mentioned earlier, it's important not only to prospect at the same time every day, but in the *exact same way* every day. Have a script for every category of prospects you could possibly be calling: FSBOs, Expireds, Just Listeds, Just Solds, Past Clients, Sphere of Influence, ABC List, etc. Incidentally, on a daily basis, that's a good order in which to do your actual prospecting.

Your script would be some form of *"Who do you know that wants to buy or sell real estate?"* Obviously, the FSBOs and Expireds already have a known real estate need, so in that case, you'll be sure to use the two critical questions:

➢ *"Where are you moving?"*

➢ *"When do you need to be there?"*

Remember that these are used in every prospecting call to an actual decision maker to determine their motivation to sell. Once that is established with a FSBO or Expired, just get the appointment. Don't be tempted to tell them your whole listing presentation over the phone. Just empathize, tell them you're getting your clients' homes sold, and assure them you can get theirs sold, too.

If you're new and don't have any listings yet, say *"we're getting our clients' homes sold,"* meaning your office collectively. Avoid any temptation to let them lead you into a conversation about how ticked off they are at their previous agent, or in the case of the FSBO, about how much they don't like real estate agents.

SCRIPTING FSBO'S AND EXPIREDS

Write out your script, type it, laminate it, and use it *always*. Ask lots of questions:

- Where are you moving?
- When do you need to be there?
- How did you establish your price?
- How are you promoting your home?
- How many showings have you had?
- Have you had any offers?
- Why didn't you accept the offers?

Again, all of this is to help you determine motivation, and to get clues as to how long it will be before they give up and list with you.

Motivation is a crucial piece of information in making your decision on whether or not you want the listing. The higher the price, the lower the motivation. There are some people who will take anything, at any price, and do very well in their business. Maybe they have a great system that makes them masterful at getting price reductions.

I personally won't take the listing unless:

- It's priced right.
- It's in saleable condition.
- The Seller is attitudinally reasonable.

That's because I've been at this nearly twenty-five years, have made every mistake there is, and could write a separate book on the resulting war stories. Over-priced listings just *do not sell*. The buying public will not over pay just because we have a difficult Seller. Over-priced listings cost a lot of money to promote, and a lot of emotional energy to maintain. Just make yourself a cardinal rule not to take them. If you commit to a serious prospecting habit, you won't have to.

SIX FIGURE INCOME

The telephone is the most inexpensive and efficient method of prospecting, and incidentally, it's a myth that people will be rude to you. That will happen maybe six times in a whole year, which is miniscule as a percentage.

THE CALL THAT'S MOST CRITICAL

One of my favorite prospecting stories goes way back to one of the earliest years we were in Flagstaff, and I didn't know many people yet. I was using the phone book and came upon the name of 'Larry and Arlene.' Larry and I were on a service club board together, and I knew he was friends with the President - fishing buddies, no less. I thought I couldn't call him because the President's sister was in the real estate business and partnered with one of *the* top agents in town.

I skipped over Larry and Arlene and went on calling, only to be nagged by an awareness that I just flat-out didn't have the guts to make the call. This went on for about fifteen or twenty minutes and I just couldn't stand it, so I finally made the call. Larry, himself, answered and told me they didn't have any real estate needs right then, but they'd *"keep me in mind."* You get a lot of that, so I thought, *See, what'd I tell you?*

About two or three months later, Larry called and explained that their son and daughter-in-law were moving back to town, and he wondered if I'd help them buy a house. Pretty cool, huh? Well, it gets *better*. The day we found the house they bought, standing in the house making a plan to go to my office and write the contract, Larry said that he and Arlene wanted to talk to me *"sometime"* about a new house. The way he said *"sometime"* sounded sort of vague, and I thought he meant one of those later on down the road deals. I asked him when they'd like to do that, and you can imagine my surprise and delight when he looked at his watch and said, *"Could you come by after you finishing writing the kids' contract?"* Wow! And I *almost* didn't make that call!

I ended up selling Larry and Arlene's house myself, so I had two 'sides' there, sold them another home, sold their kids that first town home which I sold again two years later and put them in *another* home. On top of *that,* the people who bought Larry and Arlene's house didn't stay long, so I sold that again the next year. That's a lot of business from just one prospecting call. Is it important to call *everybody* you know? You *bet* it is. Don't fall into the trap of disqualifying people. Unless somebody is either licensed themselves, married to an agent, or the blood relative of an agent, *they are a prospect,* at least as far as calling is concerned. Make the call.

At the very least, the people you call, even if they never have a real estate need, will respect you because that type of prospecting is not common. A lot of people think real estate agents sit in a snazzy office, dressed to the hilt, drive around in their spotless late-model luxury cars, don't do much actual work, and are rewarded by staggering sums of money. When they see somebody really working at getting business they remember it. The next time someone mentions they're going to be moving, your name will come up. There are some things you can do to make sure it does, such as developing your 'Everybody I Know List' and your ABC list, and simply calling to ask for their help like 'Bob' in our earlier story does.

All great agents have some system of doing this, and it doesn't have to be a tedious chore. If you work twenty days a month and call only five people a day from each of these lists, you'll make twelve hundred of this type of call a year. If you have a list of three hundred people, you'll obviously call each one four times a year. That's not being a pest, it's telling them you're committed and serious and they *will* respect you for it. Your name will come up each and every time somebody says they're looking for a hard working agent. After a period of doing this, you'll get a ton of referral business.

Remember to thank everybody for their referrals. There are a lot of ways to do this, but I've already mentioned that I really like personal handwritten notes on beautiful high quality cards. Nobody does this anymore. We call or email, so a handwritten note on a nice card with a commemorative stamp makes a great statement and is remembered. I've had a lot of people call and thank me for my thank you note just because it is such a nice thing to do.

Remember these people, too, socially whenever you can. Some people will be naturals and will fit comfortably in your expanded circle of friends. For those who don't, you may want to send them tickets to an event or a special movie, again with a nice note thanking them for remembering you. I know a young couple who have an annual event for all the people they want to thank for sending them business or personally doing business with them. They buy a big block of tickets for a holiday play and invite us all to attend. They don't even have to spend any money for refreshments, because the local play house provides them. Besides the mileage they get out of thanking their strongest supporters, the theater company loves them for boosting attendance, and they get a lot of referral business from the people involved in the theater productions.

Door-Knocking Without Doors

Although telephone calling is the least expensive and most time-efficient method of prospecting, there's another method that's almost in the same category, and that's door-knocking. Now see... your heart's racing, right? Or maybe you've just thrown this book against the wall in protest. Nothing invokes such panic as the suggestion of door-knocking.

I've never actually been personally acquainted with anyone who did massive amounts of it. Like you, I've just heard the legends of the super-human mega agents who are *rumored* to do two, four, occasionally even six hours of it daily. Frankly, I've never believed many people have the stomach for that either, even when it's done in blitz fashion in a group.

Back when I did formal door-knocking, per Mike Ferry's relentless instruction, it always felt intimidating. I used to door knock with my friend 'Lisa.' We always said we did it together for security reasons, but in truth, I suspect it was really because without a partner, neither of us would have gone through with it.

In the earliest years of my real estate career, I did a different type of door-knocking and didn't even realize what it was. My first broker, 'John,' was a six-foot-five attorney, with a deep booming voice, intimidating presence, and a size fourteen shoe. He gave me all my initial training in one day. On the morning of my first day, he told me to go preview all of the company's listings. Small town, small office, it was easily accomplished that first morning. That afternoon, I came back and John said, *"Now I want you to leave the office and don't come back until you have a listing, a sale, or somebody you're sure you can either list or sell."* Period. That's it. John was never one for ceremony. That was the *best* lesson I ever had. I was scared to find out if he meant it.

Well, Vermillion had no industry, and only one real major employer: The University of South Dakota. One advantage of a small town is that you *really do* know everybody. So I went up to the University, and literally started going from one department to the next talking to secretaries, faculty, department heads, you name it. My question was, *"Are any of your people moving?"* It was easy. I knew everybody, and because they knew me, they were more than glad to help. If anybody had called it 'door-knocking,' I probably would have frozen with terror, but I thought I was just talking to friends while I was looking for business.

How Can You Make This Work For You?

First, take a look at who you know, and think about all the organizations you currently belong to. I'd recommend that you:

- Join the Chamber of Commerce
- Look in the Chamber Directory to see who you know
- Group five or six businesses located in the same area
- Stop by for just a minute or two
- Go early in the day before they get tied up
- You don't need to take anything except your business card
- Ask for business: Who in their company is moving?
- Ask if they're hiring

Always take your business card, present it the minute you arrive, and make it clear why you're there. If you're not going through a couple of thousand cards a year, you're not prospecting enough.

Just ask: *"Are you hiring? When? How can I help? I'll be glad to provide information and take the spouse around and sell them on the community while you sell the candidate on the job."*

John left town after my first year, and I worked for nine years with my friend, 'Sarah,' who still owns a successful real estate company in Vermillion, and is still a good friend. Sarah has an extraordinary work ethic, taught me a lot, and opened a lot of doors for me at USD. In a few years, I literally *owned* the relocation business of the Athletic Department, the ROTC unit, the Law School, the School of Business, and two departments in the Medical School.

In other situations, if you're working on a small business that usually hires locally, you might take a few flyers of your latest listing and just tell them you're looking for a Buyer. Ask if they know anyone who wants to move. Remember Howard Brinton's sage advice and go three deep with your prompts:

➤ *"How about anybody else here at work?"*

➤ *"What about anybody in your car club?"*

➤ *"What about anybody at your church?"*

Whenever you first start approaching anybody in this manner, their reflexive reaction *will* be, *"I don't know of anybody,"* so tell them you'll check in with them every three months or so. My favorite phrase for such situations is **"With your permission** *I'll touch base in a few months."* Nobody says no, that you can't call them again. Then tag your scheduler with a 'tickler,' and of course, it'll be for *two months* so you can contact them minimally six times a year.

As I mentioned, when I did all that door-knocking to launch my career in 1977, I didn't even know it was 'door-knocking,' which is probably why it worked so well. There was *no intimidation factor*. I thought I was just going around talking to people looking for business, which is precisely the mindset you need when engaged in that kind of activity. I really do feel there is a huge difference between this and conventional door-knocking that involves going door-to-door in a neighborhood.

That can be a highly successful method of prospecting but this is so much easier. Understand, it's the exact same activity, but it *feels* a lot different. Part of it is because we know going in that the chances of getting a door slammed in our face is dramatically reduced. People want to look professional in front of their colleagues, after all.

We talked about the ABC list awhile back. To expand on that, create your list by making an alphabetical list of every profession you can think of; then go through and put a name to each. You don't think you can call your doctor, your dentist, or your accountant? Why not? If you do business with them, it is perfectly reasonable for you to ask them to do business with you.

Again, practice what you're going to say so you won't fumble around and get your message out. Don't add it as an *"Oh, by the way . . ."* or you won't be taken seriously. By all means, have a minute or so of chatting pleasantly in greeting, as you normally do when you see that person, but if you throw it out at the end, just as you're leaving, it'll lose its impact. If you bring it out the minute you've exchanged greetings, the conversation will take a whole different turn. Attitudinally, they'll view the call favorably, and their mindset will be *"Wow! No wonder she's so good at her business, she talks to people about it all the time."* or, *"Gosh, he's dedicated."* Once you get people reacting in this mindset, you're on your way.

I once had an interesting thing happen back in the Vermillion days regarding this very situation. I was at the ROTC department at USD, and my good friend, 'Nancy,' whom I'd helped get into a house when they came to town, was there waiting for her husband, who was the headest of honchos in the department. Imagine my surprise when I came out of the Colonel's office just in time to hear Nancy say to someone, *"Let me put in a word with Sue for you. She does **all** the University's relocation business, and I want to make sure you get her, personally."* Ta Da! When it works right, that's how it's supposed to work. As soon as you get a few people thinking this way, and treat the business they send you with great respect, and treat your relationship with *them* with great respect, your business will grow and flourish, and you'll have great fun with it. Incidentally, I did *not* do all the University's relocation business by any stretch of the imagination, but that was Nancy's perception, which is precisely the goal.

So...can you do that? No matter what level you're at now, you can do that. If you couldn't, you wouldn't be in the real estate business, and if you weren't pretty good at it, or confident that you're going to *get* good at it, you wouldn't be reading a book about how to make a nice income, living your life the way you want. I've given you several examples of the various methods of prospecting, and told you several true-life stories to illustrate them, because my goal for you is to find a way to prospect that will not be so tedious and intimidating that you don't do it. All of these methods can be done by anybody in any market, at any level of experience, and at any career level. All it takes is the basic preparation and the firm commitment that it will be done on a daily basis.

If you've been in the business quite awhile, you can't very well go to your beauty shop as say, *"I need your help. I'm new to the real estate business and I'm looking for people who want to buy and sell homes."* But there is always something new and interesting going on in the industry and you can certainly use some of those things as your approach. Tell them about a new loan program that is especially helpful to first time buyers, or a program that really benefits investors, or take a flyer with your newest listing. Tell them how excited you are and ask if they know anyone you should sent it to. You'll probably do hand springs the first time your hair stylist responds with, *"How much do you think we could get for our house? We've kind of been talking about a new home, and I **love** this area."* Do this. Do a lot of it. It *really* works.

What we're talking about here comes under the category of 'door-knocking,' but it's really just a matter of developing the habit of talking to people all the time, everywhere you go, about real estate.

'Door-Knocking' Everywhere You Go

The important thing to focus on is:

- ➤ Do it with a plan
- ➤ Do it with purpose
- ➤ Know what you're going to say
- ➤ Be very clear on the goal

Develop the list of people you know, the ABC list, your past clients, colleagues in organizations, *everyone* you know, and have a system of contacting them on a regular basis. You decide whether it's going to be monthly, bi-monthly, quarterly, or whatever. Some of your lists will be contacted more frequently than others, depending on how well you know them.

With the ABC list, you'll be well received every time, even if it takes awhile before you actually start getting leads, but make that list huge so you have a better chance of getting leads early on.

With the major employers who will be bringing in people most frequently, and moving people out most frequently, the reception may not be as friendly...until you get them trained. What would you do if you got in to see the big honcho and he behaved as though you had a lot of nerve looking to his company for business, and all but implied he didn't want you to come back? First of all, this won't happen very often, but *if it did* what would you do? Would you just never go back and miss all that business? Of course not. You'd go when you felt certain you could talk to the receptionist or the administrative assistant, or better yet, *both*.

They're the ones who are going to coordinate all the activity surrounding the candidates who come in to interview. If you offer to take them around for an overview of the town and to any points of personal interest, they'll schedule you in. They know that anything the employer can do to look good to the candidate is a good thing, and by arranging it for the employer, they know they'll make themselves look good, so you see, *everybody* wins.

On the next two pages, we'll look at a re-cap of the things we've discussed here, in an Overview of the Goals of Prospecting, and in a form you can use as a daily call sheet to help you stay on track.

Overview Of The Goals Of Prospecting

① Looking For New Clients:

- Right Now Business (People with a known need)
- For Sale By Owners
- Expired Listings
- Future Business (People to put in your database)
- Just Listed Neighbors
- Just Sold Neighbors
- ABC List
- Sphere List

② Follow-up on Leads after they're identified:

- Right Now: Regular Scheduled and Systematic Calls
- Future: Database Management
- By Letter: Done by your assistant
- By Phone/In Person: Done by you personally
- In both cases, contact management program will prompt

③ Building Repeat and Referral Business:

- ABC List
- Sphere List
- Past Clients

DAILY PROSPECTING LOG

Date: _____

FSBOs and Expireds:

_____ _____
_____ _____
_____ _____
_____ _____
_____ _____

Just Listed and Just Sold:

_____ _____
_____ _____
_____ _____
_____ _____
_____ _____

ABC List and Sphere:

_____ _____
_____ _____
_____ _____
_____ _____
_____ _____

Past Clients and Major Employers:

_____ _____
_____ _____
_____ _____
_____ _____
_____ _____

(Six Figure Income / Sue Christensen ©2002 All Rights Reserved)

Notes:
_____
_____
_____
_____
_____
_____
_____

The best thing that happened during prospecting today was:
_____
_____
_____
_____
_____
_____
_____

Calls Completed: _____

Appointments Scheduled: _____

Time Spent: _____

Today was _____% successful.   Signed: _____

(Six Figure Income / Sue Christensen ©2002 All Rights Reserved)

Chapter Five
Taking Control Of Your Time

The Magic of The Five Day Week

One of the most important life lessons and best pieces of advice I've ever gotten in my real estate career came from Mike Ferry, the first time I heard him speak in 1991. Until then I felt that to be successful, I had to be on call *all the time.* Mike, who is the single most focused and disciplined individual I have ever met, said, *"Work however many hours you want and need to, but **do it in five days**."*

He advised us to give some serious thought to which two days would be our days off, and make a commitment to stick to them. Working seven days a week as a continuous matter of habit will burn anybody out of any job, obviously, but that's what I'd done in my first ten years. Most good agents do, at least in the early stages. We're afraid that if we're not there, somebody else will be and we'll miss the opportunity to make the sale. That's why it's critical to make the decision of your scheduling very thoughtfully. For me, the decision was easy. I work Monday through Friday, and have for the last eleven years, because the weekend is when the special people in my personal life are available for fun.

Most of us are pre-conditioned to believe we have to work weekends when people are off work and can buy homes, so if you decide Saturday and Sunday are your days off, it may seem scary at first. It did to me. But over the eleven year period that I've done it, it's *worked,* and I've always been grateful to Mike for this liberating piece of advice.

First, I want to be very clear. I am *not* telling you to make Saturday and Sunday your days off. That's a very personal decision, but once those days off are determined, get them in your scheduler as 'booked.' The next person who requests an appointment on those days is told that you're 'booked solid.' Practice this several times before you have the dialog with a live prospect. You'd never want to just come right out and say you simply don't want to work that particular day, or it'll come out sounding like you're not interested in doing business with them. Their reply will be some form of, *"Fine, I don't want to do business with you either,"* and a pattern of conversations like that won't build a solid client base and a successful business.

We're in Northern Arizona, where it's 78 to 85 degrees in the summer, when it's 110 or worse in Phoenix, where a lot of our second home Buyers come from. Here's what has been working well for me:

> Prospect: *"We can come up Saturday to look at homes."*
>
> My Reply: *"Gosh, I'm booked solid Saturday, but I don't want to keep you waiting. What about Friday afternoon? Do you have any time open then?"*

You'd be *amazed* at the number of times people will say, *"Well sure; I usually take off at noon on Friday any way." But you have to ask.* Sometimes they'll say, *"No, I'm only available to come up on weekends."* Remember Howard Brinton's advice to *"go three deep,"* meaning ask again for an alternative time, then a third time before accepting their suggested time.

Your response will be to tell them that you're looking ahead to the next few weekends to see if you have any openings. You already know you don't, because you've physically filled in the entire year in your scheduler, and you are indeed, booked solid.

Again, we don't want to seem insensitive, so we're going to say:

> *"I'm looking ahead to the next two weekends and I see I am booked completely solid then too, but I see there's _____ coming up,"* (Veterans' Day, Presidents' Day, there are a lot of those extra Mondays scattered throughout the calendar). *"Will you be off that day?"*

With practice, once you've developed the mindset of *exactly* what days you work, and really commit, you'll be amazed how frequently you do get the appointment, when initially it looked like it just wouldn't click.

There will be times when you've gone *three deep* looking for a mutually agreeable time slot and it just can't be done. Then you've got a decision to make. My advice to you is *refer them to another agent.* A twenty-five percent referral fee for a thirty-minute conversation is a beautiful thing.

Give some thought to who, among your peers, you'd like to have such an arrangement with. It obviously can't be somebody whose main method of prospecting is weekend Open Houses, or somebody who travels a lot, so pay attention to who does what, and you'll know who is your primo refer to agent. In a perfect world, you'd have somebody who takes off Wednesday and Thursday, then you could refer back and forth and you'd both be happy. Look for that, too. It's amazing how often the exact situation you're looking for is right there...but you have to ask.

When you're referring someone out, after the three-deep probe, take great care in how you do it. Done right, you may make the favorable impression that will get you the listing in three, four, or five years when that Buyer becomes a Seller, and the agent you referred them to has moved on. This happens *all the time*. If you're marketing yourself right (we'll talk more about that later), the prospect will know you're still at the same office or where you've moved.

Most people in a second-home market, where they live elsewhere, unless they've developed a

Six Figure Income

friend in the business, will return to the office where they made the purchase. Years ago, before we got better at marketing ourselves, people wouldn't necessarily remember the name of their agent, but they'd gravitate back to that office only to be grabbed up by the 'Floor Agent,' so there are two lessons here:

- If you sold the prospect, make sure you remind them frequently.
- If *any* agent moves or gets out of the business, go in your office files, get the names of those now agent-less clients and get them in your database.

Your broker will let you do this. She'll also respect you for recognizing the opportunity in those abandoned files, and appreciate your efforts to keep that business in-house.

It does seem a little risky at first when you go to the five-day work week, but believe me, it will serve you well in the long run. I've often wondered if there was a correlation between this and the outrageously high turnover in our industry. With seventy to eighty percent of the people who enter the real estate business leaving after just a couple of years, we know that's not traditional burn out. Another kind, perhaps, but I'd guess it's more likely due to frustration at being directionless in the attempt to be at everybody's beck and call all the time, and never having a personal life.

That's what this book is all about. It's about making a great income, but making smart decisions about how you're going to run your business and how you're going to live your life. This isn't going to be about creating a mega, off-the-charts real estate practice. It's about making a consistent six figure income and living a nice life, where real estate is what you do, not who you are. I've always said my competitors would have a fit if they knew my work schedule and realized that I just simply do *not* work nights and weekends. Period. And yet, for these last several years, I've continued to remain one of the top agents in town.

Be Responsible

Obviously, this means I work with a lot more Sellers than Buyers, and that responsibility has to be taken seriously. No Seller should ever be at risk of missing an opportunity to show their home and get it sold just because we're having a day off. It is vital to make sure people have access to our listings *all the time*. Granted, Saturday and Sunday off have greater potential to make Sellers mad than Monday or Tuesday, again due to pre-conditioning; but the fact is, people do have days off, and a provision has to be made to anticipate that.

My advice is a pretty rigid rule:

Don't take a listing that won't allow a lock box.

Very few people will oppose this now that the industry has factored security into the design of the lock box. It only takes a few minutes to explain the importance of a lock box and how it directly relates to the number of showings they're going to have.

From what I hear at the national events I attend, most other MLS's put the Seller contact information into the system, so agents just call the Seller direct to arrange showing appointments. Flagstaff still has the system of having all showings cleared and coordinated through the Listing Agent's office. I've always thought that was an unnecessary layer of management, but that's the policy, so I put my cell phone number in the comments and showing instructions, and make sure I carry my phone and my list of client numbers with me at all times.

Once you have a showing scheduled for a particular day, ask your Seller to be alert to the possibility of others, then the next agent to call can be told to proceed without the need for another call. I've been doing this for quite awhile, and I'm comfortable in the belief that my days off are not an obstacle to my clients' ability to get their homes shown.

Now that we've talked about the five-day work week, we should address the number of hours. This too, is somewhat personal, but remembering that what we're talking about here in not just *being in the real estate business,* but making a strong, consistent *six figure income.* It should be obvious that a significant amount of work has to be done. There's a price for *everything.* If people could make six figures without doing much, everybody would be doing it. There's no way in this industry to make a lot of money without a strong work effort. But I'd much rather do it this way and take my two days off. If your market is seasonal, you'll have certain times of the year where you'll work longer and harder than others.

Personally, I like to view 7:00 to 7:00 as available work hours. There's a lot of time that it may not be necessary to start until 8:00 or 8:30, and a lot of time, it works to stop at 5:00 or 6:00, but scheduling between 7:00 and 7:00 is a good overall concept. Naturally, you'll want to try, whenever possible, to schedule in order, so you don't have one appointment at 7:00 a.m. and another at 6:00 p.m. with nothing in between.

You'll need some help. You can't do everything by yourself or you won't do much business. Think of it this way: if you have one assistant who works eight hours a day, and you've worked twelve, that's *twenty hours* worth of work that got done that day, and you *still* went home at 7:00, had dinner with your family, and spent the evening together. So relating back to my point earlier that there's a price for everything; I'd much rather pay ten dollars an hour for someone to help me, than pay the price of missing dinner and an evening with my family.

Don't Over-complicate It.

I personally am not real wild about multiple assistants, or a big team, although I have a lot of respect for the strong producers who do well with them. Been there, done *both,* and that's not for me, so it's not the subject of this book. I have the heart and soul of a salesperson, and I'm a flaming entrepreneur, not a manager, and it's not pretty when I do it anyway. Know yourself and be true to yourself in this regard.

SIX FIGURE INCOME 49

I am a huge fan of Lauren Harper-Haden, who does sixty-plus transactions a year with one assistant she's had for about nine or ten years now. Lauren does very well and has an admirably balanced life. She's pretty much always been the agent I've kept my eye on and tried to learn from because she's resisted the temptation to over-complicate. Lauren is a consistent strong producer with RE/MAX in the Chicago suburban area, and she has video programs to share her system with others, which I highly recommend. The point obviously, is she does all this with *one* assistant, *and* she has a personal life.

Now more than ever, I *know* there is an audience waiting for this book. Everywhere I go, I continue to see more and more successful people who are looking for Life Balance. The people I go around with are almost all, with few exceptions, hard-charging entrepreneurs who are very successful. They are people whose success has been influenced by their work effort and their willingness to pay the price of success. But more and more, regardless of our level of success, we have come to realize that the one price we are *not* willing to pay, is the sacrifice of our *life*. We are *all* seeking life balance.

We've come to realize that we need to set boundaries. Some are small and easily established, such as: all calls during dinner go to voice mail. Others, for some of us will include the decision of whether or not to take regularly scheduled days off or multiple days' vacation.

I used to think, years ago, that it was a big deal that I'd sold homes on Memorial Day, Labor Day, 4th of July, New Year's Eve, etc. I thought that in making this boast, I'd win the respect and approval of those whom I wanted to see me as a highly successful, dedicated professional. Now I'm no longer proud of having made sales on days that should have been family days, and that's a mistake I'd *never* repeat today, even with an average commission of over $5,000.

I've re-assessed my priorities and now, even putting myself in the *position* of making sales on family days, is simply no longer an option. I'm already booked solid on those days, and frankly, I don't think I've lost much, if any, business because of it. If I have, and life continues to go on just fine, as far as I'm concerned, that's just additional proof that I didn't *need* the business I might have had on those days.

WORK ISN'T LIFE, IT'S WHAT WE DO TO FUND LIFE

I was in a break-out session at a major conference, and the topic was Life Balance. The moderator went around the room and asked everyone how many days off we'd taken the previous year. My answer was 135, figuring Saturday and Sunday for fifty two weeks, holidays, and vacations. I'm much more proud of that than I am of the holidays I worked back in the 70's and 80's before I understood that work isn't *life*, it's what we do to *fund* life. Some of the others in the group gave answers indicating that they'd taken off seven, ten, twenty days (in the *entire* year). One lady even said *zero*. Of course, all eyes were on me with the question, *"What do you do about Open Houses?"* I thought the poor lady who'd had zero days off would have to be resuscitated when I said, *"Nothing. I had my last Open House in August of 1991."* That's true, except for one time a little while back when a special client asked for one. Against my better judgment, I caved in as a personal favor just because I like her so much, and you guessed it: *two* curious neighbors were the *only* attendees. This was *with* advance publicity, good signage, and perfect weather. I rest my case.

WHEN THE VALUES ARE CLEAR, THE DECISIONS ARE EASY.

The previous story is obviously all about mindset. If you set boundaries, you will make scheduling decisions accordingly, and when your values are clear, the decisions are easy. In the eleven year period since I stopped doing Open Houses, I know of only two listings I've lost because I said *"No. I don't do them."* That's not a big price to pay for having everybody in my family *know, really know because my actions showed them* that on Sunday, *they* are truly my priority. Incidentally, even the special client in the story above would have been turned down had my husband not been out of town the week end of her request.

There's a fast food restaurant out at the Flagstaff Mall that uses a 'Closed' sign on Sundays that simply says, *"Closed so we can stay focused on life's true priorities."* Don't you love that kind of courage? I haven't noticed people taking such offense that they don't still go there Monday through Saturday. Isn't it interesting that they seem to be doing a good business on the days they *are* open? Could it be a matter of not just *accepting,* but *respecting* the boundaries of that company?

SETTING OUR OWN BOUNDARIES

We can do the same thing as individuals. We need to *actually, physically* put 'Family Time' in our scheduler. Then, when we are asked for an appointment during that time, we can say with complete honesty: *"I'm sorry. I'm booked solid."* Remember our earlier dialog:

> *"I don't want to keep you waiting; what about Friday?"*

I'll repeat: once you start doing that, people *will* respond favorably. Remember:

> *"Sure. I usually take off at noon on Friday **anyway**."*

Can *you* get an appointment with your dentist, your doctor, your attorney, your accountant on Saturday or Sunday? Not likely. Why not? Because that's not their *business hours*. It's their *personal* time, very likely *family* time, and they've built a successful practice around those boundaries, with all of us as their clients *respectful* of those boundaries.

Have you noticed that when you do have an appointment with you doctor or dentist, your attorney or accountant, their reception areas are always full of other clients? Well, how are these people getting time off to see these other professionals during proper business hours, if the only time they can get off to look at homes is Saturday and Sunday?

Six Figure Income

See Yourself As A Professional

As soon as you see yourself at the same level as other professionals, others will see you at that level and will truly respect your time. If you don't think you can go cold-turkey, start with just *one* day. When that feels right, add a second. I don't know your market and I don't know your business, but I will tell you this: weekends off has worked for me for *over ten years*.

My observation has been that the reason so many people think the public is out buying houses on the weekend, is because *our industry* has invited it. We keep having Open Houses, and people see the signs and ads and they *think* people are showing up, and logic would suggest that if they're showing up, they're buying. People outside the industry have no idea that it's all a matter of misleading perception. We all threw out our old Smith-Coronas when times changed; why not throw out that old notion that we have to work on Sunday? Outside of a new homes subdivision, I'm not really able to equate an Open house to working, however. In my experience, with the new construction exception, it's usually a pretty passive, non-productive activity to pacify a Seller. Believe me, a few minutes of education at listing time is much better.

Helping Others Adjust Their Thinking

There is something indescribably liberating about truly taking charge of the daily habits that determine the boundaries of your life. It takes awhile to really get it down and make it as much an ingrained part of you as brushing your teeth, but once it's there, it's the greatest. It has been my observation that people who do this are noticeably happier, and less stressed than those who just *can't* let go. Give yourself a chance to go from zero to full-speed, so to speak, and expect that the people closest to you will need some conditioning and acceptance time. I'm speaking here of the few closest people whose approval you *want*. By the time you've mastered the principles of living life on your own terms, you won't *need* anybody else's approval but your own, but you'll still *want* it. The interesting thing is, the great improvements in your life will result in such positive, dynamic approval. It comes with the territory. Pretty exciting thought, isn't it?

You may have a Broker, an Office Manager, a spouse, a parent, a colleague who are all used to hitting the ground running, and arriving at the office earlier than anyone else, say 7:00 a.m. every day, including weekends, with no other day off. Even if they're the nicest persons in the world, their behavior and subtle comments may suggest that they are judgmentally assuming that whatever time you come into the office, you just got out of bed.

You know from your interaction with those persons that this attitude also carries with it *their* thought, not yours, and not reality, that you're not measuring up. They may even insinuate a suspicion that you may be lazy. Most of us would hate that thought enough to react to it by adjusting our behavior. Don't let that happen. Consider this: offices all across America are full of people at the crack of dawn, late at night, and on weekends. Other than those who have a specific appointment with someone who wants to buy or sell, someone they can learn from or teach, or someone they can have fun with, do you know why they are there? Because that's what they think they need to do to gain acceptance and approval. And make no mistake about it, at varying levels that's what every single one of us is looking for. It is our quest in life to be loved and accepted. Period. Everything we do is leading up to that one very basic and compelling need.

We all believe that what the folks at home *really* mean by saying *"Bob is at the office"* is that Bob is:

- Responsible

- Honest

- Hard-working

- Doing something important

These are all qualities that are valued in our culture, so we assume that if we do them routinely, we'll be respected, and therefore, loved and accepted. Maybe that's got as much to do with so many salespeople's reluctance to take a day off as the fear of lost business.

You'd think that after six months or a year of never making a sale or taking a listing on a Saturday, or making so few sales that it's just not worth drifting away from the family, people would stop doing it. But in the real estate industry, that is simply not the norm...except with the people who are doing the most business.

The Three Keys To A 'Day Off'

There are three simple things you need to do to take a day off. Again, I'll repeat, I am not telling you to take off Saturday and Sunday. I just continue to use that example because those have been my days off for the last eleven years.

- First: Make the decision and educate everybody around you.

- Second: Make a proper provision so nobody is neglected.

- Third: Be *ruthless* in protecting your day off.

It really is that simple, and I absolutely guarantee, your life will be so much more pleasant you won't believe it.

Let's elaborate on these three principles. Making the decision should address your personal relationships and the nature of your business. Again, the people I want to spend my days off with are folks who work Monday through Friday, so that was a no-brainer for me. Also, I had learned from experience about the idiocy of Open Houses in the resale market, which is primarily where I work. Thus, it became very easy for me to embrace the value of a full, productive Monday through Friday schedule, which would completely justify taking weekends off.

Remember that in educating people about your boundaries, you need to pay careful attention to *their* needs and feelings. Over the years, I've heard a number of really good agents tell their prospects in response to a request for an appointment that's outside of their boundaries:

> *"That's not how I work."*

> *"Let me tell you how I work."*

I still cringe when I hear that, even though I was in the same seminar where that was taught. It sounded disrespectful of the client at the instruction level, and it sounds worse in the real world. For me, this feel better and has always worked:

> *"I'm sorry. I'm booked solid."*

> *"But I don't want to keep you waiting."*

It shows no lack of regard for the client's needs and establishes very clearly that the particular day they're requesting is *not an option*. It's already booked. I have also found that in telling them I never like to keep people waiting and probing a little bit (by going three deep) for other days they either have available or can make available, is just a positive, caring way of handling a very common problem in real estate. Remember, our industry has invited this, so it's up to those of us who are fiercely determined to have a successful personal life *and* a successful career, to change this myth, one client at a time.

With the age-old Open House thing, that's a different story and has to be handled differently. If you say you're booked solid, they'll just go weeks and weeks out in their request to be scheduled. My advice is to provide the answer before the question comes up. Tell them what you do to market homes and get them sold. Then say:

> *"I'm sure you're as busy as everybody else, and I know you'll be relieved that I'm not going to kick you out of your house on Sunday afternoon, just to parade a few neighbors through so they can see how you've decorated."*

In most cases, in fact, *in an overwhelming majority of cases,* the clients will say, *"Oh, good. We think Open Houses are so stupid."* Practice. Practice. Practice. Know what you're going to say, internalize it into your belief system, and the conviction *will* be there when you need to have that conversation.

> **'No Open House' Alternative Marketing**
>
> Be sure to tell them how much greater value there is in making it easy for the other agents to have access by means of:
>
> - MLS caravan/tour
> - Agent Open House lunch
> - Being on a lock box
> - Being on *Show Anytime* status

The 'F' Word in Real Estate: Floor Time

Now, insofar as educating the people around you, if you're in a traditional office that still has floor time, you need to talk to your Broker, and tell him that you won't be taking floor time *any* day, much less weekend days. If you're lucky and you're in a big office where there are still plenty of people who want floor time, this won't be an issue. But if that's not the case, and your Broker throws a fit, *leave now,* and go where it won't be a problem.

I'm not going to debate whether offices all across the country should or should not have floor time. That's a philosophical question, and I'm not trying to change every office in America. I'm just trying to change *you*. My goal is to help you become a highly productive agent, making a lot of money and having a lot of fun, who has a very satisfying personal life. This *really works*. You just have to *do* it, so you need to believe in it.

Do You Have A Job, Or A Business?

The second consideration in having two days off, especially weekend days, is making a provision for business to continue in your absence that we mentioned briefly earlier. Obviously, you've concluded by now that you're working with more Sellers than Buyers, which has worked so well for me and for lots of others, and does make time management much more predictable. If you're going to take a listing on somebody's house, you have to accept the fact that until you get that house sold and closed, they can't go anywhere and can't move forward with their plans. There are several ways to properly address this huge responsibility:

Six Figure Income

- Have a Buyer Agent

- Refer out all buyers to an 'On Call' agent

- Put the house on 'Show Anytime' status

If you have a Buyer Agent or more than one Buyer Agent, somebody would be on call seven days a week. Another way to do this is to refer out all Buyers to another agent who is on call all the time. A much simpler way is to clear it with your Seller that they'll get the best exposure if they're on a 'show anytime' status, then put this in the MLS system comments along with *"Please knock before entering."*

What about people who are cruising around and call on your yard sign? Have a sign rider with a cell phone number, other than your personal cell phone. This separate cell phone has voice mail, and your message tells the caller that you'll be in Monday at 7:00 a.m. (that means you personally or your assistant) and will return their call promptly, or if they want to see the house right away, they can go to www.whatever for a virtual tour, or they can call Agent X, who is on call. This separate cell phone is your 'Money Line' and anytime it rings, you know it's a sign call or an ad call, because those are the only places this number appears. If you have Buyer Agents, have them rotate carrying it every day so it's answered live from 7:00 to 7:00. Outside of those hours, most people will be fine with voice mail.

Also, having great flyers in the box on the sign and making sure you keep the flyer box filled is an excellent way to provide round-the-clock information. Put the price on the flyer. Don't make people call for the price. You do not want those calls. You want calls from people who *know* the price and want to *buy* the house. Do your job prospecting and you'll have a lot of listings, which will result in a lot of calls. Do everything you can to make them *quality* calls.

135 Days and 365 Nights Off

Finally, the third component of getting two days off: *Be ruthless in protecting them*. This isn't as hard as it may sound, but it does take practice. The first really critical step in doing this is to put them into your scheduler, electronic or otherwise. By scheduling your days off a full year in advance, you're automatically doing several things at once: you're also scheduling your days on, so you can calculate the number of hours you have available each month, week, and day for revenue-instigating (prospecting) and revenue-generating (working with clients) appointments.

You can match up those hours with the number of listings you need to meet your financial goals, and by paying attention to your numbers, you'll know how many people you have to talk to for that number of appointments. You'll know how many appointments to get a listing, how many of those listings have to close to get to the bank with a deposit, etc.

All of these things relate back to the amount of time available and the amount of time spent on each activity. If you've never tracked your numbers, start immediately. I'll give you two to get started: you should be able to talk to fifteen people in an hour when you're telephone prospecting. You should allow an hour and a half for a listing appointment. That's fifteen minutes commute time each way (adjust if you need more), and no more than an hour at the house. That's from *"Hi, thanks for inviting me over today,"* to *"Thank you very much; I'll have my sign contractor install the sign tomorrow, and I'll get you on the internet today."*

YOUR MODEL DAY

I encourage you to give some serious thought to your Model Day, meaning your model of perfection for a work day. I have five things that are very important to me that need to be done before the end of the traditional noon hour, so scheduling is critical.

EXAMPLE MODEL DAY

Here's what my Model Day looks like:

6:00 a.m.	30 Minutes on the Treadmill
6:30-8:30	Two Hours of Writing
8:30-9:30	Shower/Hair/Make-up
9:30-10:30	Phone Prospecting
10:30-11:00	Commute to Office (Errand or two)
11:00-11:45	Misc: Return Calls/Meet with Assistant
12:00-12:45	M-W-F Work Out with My Trainer
1:00-6:00	Available for Client Appointments
1:00	_____
2:00	_____
3:00	_____
4:00	_____
5:00	_____
6:00	_____
7:00-10:00 p.m.	Available for Personal and Family Time.

> ## YOUR MODEL DAY
>
> What does your Model Day look like? I think it's important to give this some serious thought and get it on paper where you can really look at it.
>
> ➤ Spend a couple of days with it
>
> ➤ Move things around as your thoughts evolve
>
> ➤ Visualize living with it on a daily basis
>
> Does it look like it will allow you the time you need to remain highly productive, while paying careful attention to the things that really matter to you?

Look again at my Model Day. You'll see immediately that two non-real estate things are very important to me: physical fitness and writing. In my planning and scheduling, it is absolutely paramount that both of these happen early in the day. I need the assurance that the day won't fill up without having allowed for both of these things. Hair and nails may very well have to wait for a day off, but the critical things need to be scheduled and the appointment is never broken, any more than any other business appointment.

Section III:
Running a Smooth Operation

Chapter Six:
Delegation And Outsourcing

This is the point where the nay-sayers are bringing up to you: *"What about closings? What about home inspections? What about paper work? What about servicing listings? What do you do about all that?"* The answer is very simple: Nothing. Your assistant does all of that. You do not do anything except:

- Prospect
- List
- Sell
- Negotiate

That's it. *Everything else* is delegated. Regular conversations with existing clients can be handled in the forty-five minute miscellaneous section of your schedule. The whole secret there is to call them before they feel they need to call you. Have a specific system in place, where you plan to call five to eight of your clients each day.

Buyers, once they've gone into escrow, will accept that when they reach that stage of their purchase, they talk to your assistant. To make sure they know you're interested and really do care about them, I suggest that you call them personally once a week for both Sellers and Buyers, and you only need a few minutes for each call.

Your assistant needs to be trained so that every time she calls a client for you, she begins with:

> *"Sue wanted you to know right away..."*

This will make it clear that every call from your office is always generated by your caring and interest in them.

I've made every mistake there is with assistants before I got it right. In truth, every assistant I've ever had had been good at some things, great at others. But I do know from experience that it's crucial that when your client receives a call from your office, they *must* know the call came from you. There is no room for an assistant to have the need to be recognized as the person who helped them. The client will know that, but since they're your client and they're going to pay you a lot of money, you must make sure they don't feel like they've been handed off or worse yet, pushed aside just because you've made the sale or gotten the listing.

Working With An Assistant

Show your assistant this section of this book, and have an in-depth conversation about it. Make sure she understands that the client *will* be able to see who is doing the work, and she *will* be valued and appreciated. I've had people praise my assistant up one side and down the other, both directly to her, and in expression to me their appreciation for all she did to hold the details of their transaction together.

Then, make sure *you* do enough for your assistant. 'Carol,' who became my closest personal friend over the years of our working together, was such an asset to me, that the respect was automatic on a level I'd never previously experienced. At her Grandmother's funeral, when meeting a number of her aunts and uncles, I introduced myself as Carol's friend from work. I overheard her Mom telling them that I was Carol's boss. It struck me then, that although I do have to make the tough decisions and generate the money to fund the checks, I never think in terms of boss.

I suggest that you remove the word 'boss' from your vocabulary, along with the words, 'I' and 'me,' and the phrase *"works for me."* These are so foreign to my thought patterns that I find their use by others extremely offensive. I'm not sure when this started for me, but it was a very long time ago. I'm proud to say that not one single person who has ever been on my payroll can make the statement factually that they ever once heard me say I was their boss or that they worked for me. My colleagues work *with* me.

This philosophy as been a part of me for so long that years back, when my sons were in high school and got their first jobs, I explained to them that we respect and appreciate the opportunity of the job offered by our employer, but that we do *not* have a boss. I explained that this is a rather private philosophy, but that the word 'boss' is demeaning and it is simply not in our vocabulary.

My hope, of course, was that they would not arrogantly blab this around to their own detriment and to the chagrin of any employer. I also hoped that one day when they became the employer, the boss concept would be so foreign to them, that they would never run the risk of behaviors demeaning and disrespectful to their employees, whom I far prefer to think of as *colleagues.*

You can't achieve your Model Day alone, so choose your staff carefully, train them well, and always demonstrate a spirit of gratitude for all they bring to their job, and the joy with which

Six Figure Income

they perform their duties.

If you want to keep your life simple, my advice is to have only one *human* assistant. Remember, your computer and a good contact management program are another assistant. I am also a big believer in outsourcing.

Let 'George' Do It.

The single most valuable marketing I've ever done is my monthly newsletter to nine 'farms,' totaling fifteen hundred pieces. It costs about $10,000 a year, by far the most expensive single item I use, but now it returns between $40,000 and $50,000 and it's *completely outsourced.* I never touch it. In fact, I never see it until Brad brings it home, which is precisely why I have his office address in my database. Here's how it works:

My supplier ships the newsletter directly to the professional mail house here in town that processes it for me. They do everything completely, including sorting, addressing, bar coding, and physically taking all fifteen hundred pieces to the post office to mail them.

The *only* thing I do is compile the MLS data for each neighborhood, showing what's been listed, sold, and closed during the month. Then my assistant types an insert for each neighborhood and takes them to the mailing house where they are printed and inserted into each neighborhood's newsletter.

The insert is the part people really value. As far as the actual newsletter is concerned, I really don't think people care what it *says* but they do care how it *looks,* which is why I subscribe to a professionally done, high-quality, full-color product.

You know how you treat the junk mail you receive every day. So why would people treat what we send any differently? The truth is, they won't, *except* the personal stuff about *them* that you insert. The rule is:

Make a great impression while they're on their way to the trash with yours and the rest of the day's junk mail, and give them something they'll value enough to keep.

My experience has been that when I go out on a "Come List Me" call, they've saved probably one full newsletter with my contact information, but usually half a dozen or more inserts, with information about property values in their area, which they view as information *about them.*

I suppose the compiling of the MLS data for the inserts could also be delegated, but I've always continued to do this myself, because I feel it's a way to stay informed on property values, and to monitor activity.

My newsletter has been successful and has paid for itself almost from square one, and has been profitable almost as long. It takes two listing commissions to pay for mine for the entire year. I'm not sure how your numbers will work out, but you'll want to project your timeline first to break-even, then to profitability.

Getting People To Read It

Something you may want to do to increase the readership and circulation of your newsletter, is to make the back of the insert a flyer with photos and descriptions of some of your listings. Then add the phrase: *"Please Post On Bulletin Board At Work."* People may respond to your request for two reasons:

- First: They feel they're sharing something with their work colleagues.

- Second: (And by far most important): They know when *their* house is listed with you, people will be posting it on bulletin boards all over town, helping *them* gain greater exposure.

You, of course, have taken the time to put a little note on the other side to explain this.

From the very beginning, I've always gotten calls on my newsletter, even though I didn't actually get my first listing until the fourth month. Right after I sent out the first issue, I got a call from a woman who had some specific questions about some home improvements she was considering. She wondered if the market would warrant them, or if I felt she might be over-improving for the area. She began by saying, *"We've been getting your newsletter for quite awhile now, so I know you're the neighborhood expert."* I couldn't believe it. I would love to have gotten a listing right away, but frankly, that input that early was almost as valuable. That's the way it's *supposed* to work. Over time, people are supposed to see you as their area expert and come to you when they want to sell. Receiving the feedback that confirmed that perception so soon after I started the newsletter was great.

Be consistent, stick with it, and that's exactly what will happen for you. The biggest reason I advocate purchasing a professional newsletter and outsourcing the production of having it processed through a professional mail house, is so you can count on consistency.

I've known a lot of good agents over the years who have tried to do their own newsletter, and some have actually been quite well done, but it's rare to maintain consistency by doing it yourself. There are just too many things that can come up and the next thing you know, you're starting to get nervous about whether it's going to go out late, so the consistency chain is broken.

Six Figure Income

The biggest reason most people want to do it themselves is to save money. Do not fall for that very false notion. Most people, when trying to break into the six-figure bracket for the first time, can't get past the $10,000 price tag. That usually seems to be too much for just one marketing item. You do have to think this through carefully enough to believe that you're going to make it back, and get a lot of business from it. You have to know the market well enough to know there's sufficient turnover in a particular area to warrant making the investment there, Then you need to know who else is working that area and what they're doing.

The most ideal 'farm,' in my opinion, is a three year-old subdivision that sold out fast originally, and where the homes were built by a dozen or more builders. That situation will carry much less loyalty than an area done by just one builder. Realize that many of the agents who made the original sales are no longer in the business. Also, in three years, the resale will begin, and by the time you've been mailing consistently for a year or two, those four and five year old homes will be perfectly poised for a fairly significant amount of resale business.

Avoiding Panic Promotions

When you start, go in determined to outlast anybody who may decide to farm the same neighborhood. Most people are not consistent, and most do not work a big enough area or group. Mailing once-in-awhile, whether it's quarterly, seasonally, or anything less than monthly, on the *same day* each month, is just a panic promotion. That's something people do every now and then when they need more business.

You *must* mail monthly, and you *must* have a group of a thousand, *minimum.* Anything you can afford beyond that is better. You may want to start with a thousand households the first year, then add incrementally another two hundred every six months as the resulting revenues are generated. You don't pay the entire $10,000 in one shot, so you can probably figure out how to get started paying for it on a monthly basis.

Of course, your photo is right on the return address so they can see your smiling face every month, and they'll begin to feel they know you. Your web address is right there, too, and on every other marketing piece you ever use, so you are always working on driving traffic to your web site, where you can *really* show them how professional you are. Incidentally, everything connected with your web site is outsourced as well. That's really the whole key to success in a newsletter: have it all outsourced. That's the difference between something that could loom as a massive undertaking every month, and a strong income generator that you literally never have to think about.

Hiring And Training An Assistant

We've already established that when any task becomes a recurring annoyance, it's time to delegate it to someone else. We also discussed earlier that as highly productive agents, the only things we should be doing are:

- Prospect
- List
- Sell
- Negotiate

That leaves an awful lot of things that need to be delegated, and clearly points out the need for an assistant.

Most of us begin this process by creating a list of things we want an assistant to do, thereby creating a job description. There are actually two things we should explore before we get to the job description:

- Why do we need an assistant?
- What are the characteristics of a great assistant?

The *why* is obviously because we want to do a high volume business, and if we continue doing everything ourselves, that just won't happen. A top producer's number one priority is spending as much time as possible with Buyers and Sellers, and in constant search of new Buyers and Sellers.

In a sense, we need to clone ourselves, so we are always engaged in revenue generating activity, and our clone is taking care of the myriad details necessary to closing a transaction and positioning our listings so they'll be sold and eventually become closed transactions. Doubling our work effort will clearly put us in a position to do much more business than we could do alone.

One of the first areas that usually suffers when an agent needs an assistant is the follow-up work. That includes follow-up on leads, consistent follow-up with FSBOs and Expireds, and follow-up with clients you're currently working with. All of these are sources of revenue in future and Right Now business, and are far too important to be neglected.

A well-trained assistant can manage all the correspondence with everyone in your database and keep them interested in doing business with you. Your computer program tells you every day which letters go to which prospect and all you *personally* have to do is sign the letters. That's it. Your assistant does everything else toward that end, freeing you up to work with the immediate Buyers and Sellers, and to continue to prospect for new ones.

The other area that's likely to suffer while an agent is struggling to keep everything together without an assistant is prospecting. We've already established the fact that prospecting is the foundation for all else we do, the one activity that will create revenue-generating appointments.

Attending to the detail work with the intention of getting back to prospecting later is the surest way of remaining stuck at the same production level. True, all of that detail work is important, but getting caught up in it will almost guarantee that the 'later' time we intended to get back to prospecting just never seems to come.

> ### You Need An Assistant
>
> If you are finding that you're:
>
> ➢ Having trouble getting everything done
>
> ➢ Working too much
>
> ➢ Stressed out all the time
>
> ➢ Stuck at the same level
>
> ➢ Unable to increase your production

That's when you know you need an assistant. After making the decision to hire someone, or more likely, coming to the realization that we *need* to hire someone, we can begin to explore the characteristics of a great assistant.

Knowing exactly what our assistant will do will help us look at these characteristics. For example, knowing that this person will be responsible for our correspondence and tracking the progress of our listings and pending sales, we may believe the most important thing to look for is computer skills and the ability to follow through. What about the phone? Will this person answer our phone and be our first point of contact with all of our callers? If so, then a great phone voice, familiarity with generally accepted business communication skills, and friendliness and a desire to help, are an important consideration.

Let's examine exactly what we want this assistant to do, and from those requirements, we can look at essential and desired characteristics. Some of the duties of an assistant will depend on whether the person is licensed or unlicensed. Opinions vary widely on this question, but my personal preference is to hire an unlicensed person in the capacity of an office administrator.

I have two basic reasons for this: first, in the case of someone who has held a license for awhile, I prefer to avoid hiring anyone with preconceived ideas about real estate, and I don't like to try to undo anyone else's bad habits. Then, in the case of a new licensee, odds are very high that sooner or later they're going to want to try selling. That does two things: it puts us right back where we were before, without an assistant. And second, if we retain this person, we're now faced with training a sales associate, which is much different from training an assistant.

Even if the new licensee insists that there will be no selling and they simply want to be a more effective assistant, the belief that the license makes them worth more money is very difficult to explain in terms that they truly understand. In very blunt terms, the license only has value if it is indeed, used to generate revenue. Absent that, there is no more value than the contribution of the unlicensed assistant.

We could debate this indefinitely, and I realize that at some point it is possible that all of the states' Department of Real Estate may very well require licensing for assistants. For now, in today's circumstances, I personally am a proponent of the office administrator, which does not require a license.

Assistant's Job Description

Looking at the specific things we are going to ask our assistant to do, gives us a pretty good start on a job description:

Category I. Communication:

- Answer in-coming calls
- General reception duties
- Greet and welcome clients
- Manage correspondence
- Keep agent informed on all activity

Category II. Marketing:

- Write and place ads on listings
- Write and place personal promotion ads
- Prepare and distribute flyers
- Prepare newsletter insert

(continues)

Assistant's Job Description (Continued)

Category III. Tracking Listings:

- ➢ Activate new listings into MLS system
- ➢ Activate new listings into office system
- ➢ Check computer for buyer matches
- ➢ Order sign installation
- ➢ Schedule showing appointments
- ➢ Fax Agent Feed-back forms
- ➢ Seller Update Letters
- ➢ Fax paperwork for price changes
- ➢ Fax paperwork for status changes

Category IV. Tracking Escrows:

- ➢ Communication/Correspondence with other agent
- ➢ Communication/Correspondence with lender
- ➢ Communication/Correspondence with escrow officer
- ➢ Order home inspection
- ➢ Order termite inspection
- ➢ Order HOA Management documentation
- ➢ Coordinate: appraiser / movers / house cleaners / sign contractor

(continues)

Assistant's Job Description (Continued)

Category V. Follow Up:

- FSBO letters
- Expired letters
- Database letters
- Past Client letters
- Sphere of Influence letters
- Agent's Daily Phone List

Category VI. Preparation:

- Office forms
- Office supplies
- Pre-listing packages
- Listing kits
- Buyer Interview kits.

This is a general overview of the assistant's major responsibilities, and from this some of the desired characteristics are obvious. Above all else, this assistant clearly is:

- A detail person
- Able to handle multiple tasks simultaneously
- Good with people skills
- Able to work independently
- Creative enough to assist with ad writing and flyers

How Do I Find This Person?

Where do you find the person who matches this description? Before you place an ad in the paper, think about anyone you may have interacted with, who has already demonstrated that they have the skills and abilities you're looking for. The only down side to hand picking someone and pulling them off another job, is the question of how to handle the probationary period. If you're hiring the greatest real estate secretary in town away from your best competitor, you may be okay, but unless you're 99% sure of this, have a ninety day probationary period where both you and the assistant can take a good look at each other to be sure you're a good match.

Aside from personally selecting an assistant, placing an ad in your local paper is probably the way to go. Make your ad detailed, and add some verbage to make it clear that this job is a career position, not entry-level, and that it will be:

- Interesting
- Challenging
- Fast-Paced
- Creative
- Fun!

My personal philosophy on compensation is that a decent, but not over-the-top base wage should be offered, along with a great bonus schedule for the assistant's help in generating revenue through personal referrals. If this is the way you feel, the ad should also state that there is great potential for performance bonuses. And of course, the desired performance is bringing you referrals.

Reviewing the Resumes

If you place an ad, run it for two consecutive weeks and allow a full week to collect all of the resumes. Then sort through the resumes, looking for the top ten applicants. Schedule them for interviews, two a day for the entire week, and *promise yourself* that you will not hire until the *end of the week.* As a busy agent, you'll resist this, but caution here will definitely pay off in the long run.

Most of the time, in this process, we have a tendency to want to get it over with and get back to work on our production. You can still do that. The preliminary interviews are only thirty minutes, and you're only scheduling two a day.

We also sometimes have a fear that someone who appears to be a good candidate will continue looking for other jobs and will get away from us. To minimize this fear, schedule them in the order of your feeling about the strength of the resume, and keep a running Top Three file. This would include initially, the top three strongest resumes, then after each interview, ask yourself if this person is still what you'd expect in the top three candidates. After the fourth interview, select the top three, and continue through the scheduled interviews of the remaining candidates, repeating this process each time.

Making The Cut

Initially, in reviewing the resumes before going any further, those applicants who were invited to interview were the ones whose resumes were:

- Professional in appearance
- Grammatically correct
- Free of typos

The successful applicants also:

- Demonstrated a consistent, uninterrupted work history
- Stayed with each previous job a reasonable time
- Experience demonstrated compatibility with your requirements
- Were not over-qualified or over-educated for this position

I had a friend who went through a fairly lengthy period of hiring over-qualified people and was constantly having turnover problems, and being challenged by her string of assistants as to what they were and were not willing to do. When she first hired, she was always so proud that she'd found someone who was the former CEO of a company with three hundred employees, or someone who held a PhD in rocket science, or something of that nature. History just kept on repeating itself for her until she hired someone with great organizational skills, interacted well with people, and just *loved* being an office administrator.

The First Interview

In the first interview, all you're trying to do is determine a first impression and the applicant's overall attitude toward work.

The First Interview

During this time you'll want to ask them:

- About the best job they ever had
- Why they liked it
- About the worst job they ever had
- Why they didn't like it

In both cases, listen for things that you know will be similar to the job you are offering. Ask the applicant to tell you about previous relationships with employers and co-workers. If it hasn't already come out, ask if they're used to handling multiple tasks, and how they:

- Prioritize
- Organize
- Complete them

Ask how they like to work:

- Independently
- With a lot of supervision
- With minimal supervision

Pay attention to appearance and the way the applicants present themselves. How did they greet you and others in the office? This is the same way they're going to greet you and their co-workers every day, and it's how they're going to greet your clients.

I'm always interested in hearing about the authors people like and what they're reading. It's a stretch to expect an assistant who may be new to the real estate field to have done a lot of industry-related reading, but it would be interesting to know if any of the great motivational speakers and trainers are familiar to them, and hold their interest. I would at least like to know that they read regularly, irrespective of what they're reading.

> ### THE FIRST INTERVIEW (CONTINUED)
>
> You might also want to ask them about their personal interests. Ask them:
>
> ➢ What they like to do in their free time
>
> ➢ What prompted them to respond to your ad
>
> ➢ What they think they would like about working in your office
>
> The reason I prefer to ask them to tell me about various things and describe certain situations, rather than asking a lot of questions is to get them talking. I'm kind of a bugaboo about grammar and vocabulary, and this is a good way to bring out these things.
>
> Finally, ask them to tell you about:
>
> ➢ Their proudest professional accomplishment
>
> ➢ Their proudest personal accomplishment

You'll learn a lot from these answers. There may not necessarily be any pre-determined criteria for the responses, but what could be better than finding a budding artist sitting across from you, when you need an element of creativity in the person to help with your marketing pieces.

THE SECOND INTERVIEW

Think about who you will call back for a second interview *at least overnight* before making a final decision. Call the top three candidates for a second interview yourself, so you can hear their phone voice and basically, how they handle themselves on the phone.

Ask them to come in first thing in the morning, at least by 8:00, so you can see first-hand that they are either punctual or that they're on the ball enough to show up five to ten minutes early. Also, this will give you an opportunity to see if they arrive fully composed, ready to begin a productive business day, or if they rush in breathlessly as if they've had a harried time trying to get ready and arrive on time. This is one thing that's not likely to change later, and it's worth knowing how you will begin each day if you hire this person.

The second interview is the time to ask the applicants about their:

Six Figure Income

- Career Goals

- Personal Goals

Depending on their employment history and life experience, this may or may not be very detailed, and it may or may not be something they've established formally. However, it would be helpful for evaluation purposes, and ultimately for the good of your potential future relationship to know whether you're talking with someone with a nine-to-five attitude, or someone who can identify with the shaping of their own future. This will tell you more than just the predictability of long-range affiliation with your office. It will tell you where they are attitudinally:

- Do they see this strictly as a job?

- Do they see it as an opportunity for a great experience?

Now describe some of the specific duties and ask about their related abilities. Even if it has come out earlier in conversation, this is the time to ask what computer programs they know and how they used them in their previous jobs. It is also the time to ask specifically how they handled multiple-tasks and deadlines.

In describing some of the work required of the position you're looking to fill, you are also looking for instincts. In describing the process of tracking an escrow, for example, you will have explained some of the time-sensitive details. It wouldn't be fair to expect someone with no previous real estate background to know exactly how to respond, but their answers should give you some indication regarding their instinct and curiosity as to how to prioritize.

The final part of the second interview will allow you to look at actual skill level.

Begin by asking about familiarity with office equipment necessary to the performance of the required duties of the position. You already know from the candidates' resumes and from the first round of interviews that they are computer literate. Now you are ready to test the actual application by asking them to:

- Type a letter

- Create a flyer

Be prepared with an outline for the letter, a very simple three or four sentence letter with the information regarding the person to whom the letter will be sent. Have a basic description of a listing, a sample of another flyer, and show the candidate how to get into the program to create this flyer. Then give them the letterhead and envelope and leave the room while they complete both tasks. Leave the manuals for the programs on the computer desk. This, obviously, will tell you how the applicant attempts to solve the problem if the tasks are not completed fairly quickly.

In the actual performance of the job, neither of these tasks should take more than five minutes; however, allowing for probable unfamiliarity of the program for producing the flyer, ten to fifteen minutes is probably reasonable.

If the letter is to be typed in a standard word processing program, I'd be alarmed if it took much more than five minutes.

CHECKING THE ENTHUSIASM LEVEL

In the first interview when you described the position and reviewed the compensation package, you explained the bonus structure. If the applicant is serious about being hired, he or she should have been excited enough about that to have begun their sphere of influence list. A good way of finding out is to ask what have been their thoughts regarding this job in the time since their first interview. Hopefully, their response will indicate an excitement and a hope, possibly even an expectation that they will be hired. Ask if they've had any thoughts regarding their sphere list.

Even if the first candidate comes through the second interview with flying colors, *do not make a final decision* until you have completed the process with the other two top candidates. By this time, you will be able to tell them the decision will be made within two more business days, which will help relieve your fear of losing them to another job. If you've scheduled the second interviews for Monday, Tuesday, and Wednesday, each at 8:00 a.m., you'll be able to make a decision and notify the successful candidate by Wednesday afternoon.

ORIENTATION

When you've made a decision and done the actual hiring, plan for at least a full day orientation. Three half-days are actually better, if you can possibly manage, and perhaps you could put your new assistant to work on a project the other half-days while you get some of your own work done.

After a morning of orientation, you could have your assistant put together:

➢ Thirty Pre-Listing Packages

➢ Thirty Buyer Interview Kits

➢ Thirty Listing Kits

Have one of each ready, along with all the materials necessary for her to make the copies of the documents for each, and to assemble all of them. You could also have her make some flyers, and possibly make the rounds to refill the flyer boxes.

In the time you spend with your assistant during the orientation, review all office policies and procedures. Discuss dress code, and have it written out so there is no room for misunderstanding. I once had a college student as a part-time marketing assistant several years ago, and learned the hard way the importance of a written dress code. She had quite a nice wardrobe and dressed very professionally...until one day when she arrived in a very low-cut sweater that was more appropriate for a cocktail party than an office. Both of us were very embarrassed and uncomfortable when I sent her home to change. I was as gentle as possible and tried to be sensitive, but it was still awkward.

Also, early in the orientation, have some conversation about what your assistant knows about real estate agents. Ask:

- If she knows any real estate agents?
- In what way does she know them?
- What was her experience with them?
- What was her impression of them?

If she hasn't ever actually known a real estate agent, you might describe what we're *really* like. You should probably be fair enough to let her know that a busy agent may not necessarily be the easiest person in the world to work with.

Get Out Of The Way

You may not want to go so far as to tell your new assistant that we tend to be not just control freaks, but *control monsters,* but you should probably acknowledge to yourself that your biggest challenge will be letting go. Promise yourself that you will take the time to do a good job of training and be sure your assistant understands what is expected. Then let go of the tasks you delegate, and *get out of the way* and let her do her job. Understand that this is a process of shifting some of the responsibility to another person. True, you are still ultimately responsible, which is why it's important to be sure you train adequately.

We've mentioned several times the importance of having systems in place for everything. This is one of the times that those systems will be of great value. Many of the responsibilities of your assistant's job will be following a Check List for each system. This will give you a good basis for training.

Also during the orientation and training period, keep reinforcing that the reason you hired your assistant is because you could tell that she is:

- Hard-working
- A fast learner
- Self-directed

➤ Dependable

Toward the end of the first day, tell your assistant that you've ordered her business cards, and that tomorrow you're going to order the announcement card that will be sent to her sphere of influence. Ask if she has her list with her, and tell her you're planning to order two hundred of the announcement cards, if that will be sufficient. This does two things:

➤ It lets her know that a list of fifty is inadequate.

➤ It lets her know that the list is definitely due tomorrow.

It is possible that she honestly may not know that many people she could send an announcement to, but it will open a conversation where you may be able to help her.

Tell her about your ABC List and how you put it together. Ask her to work on her list first with family and friends, then with the mindset of her accountant, beauty shop, car repair place, dentist, etc. Show her with your calculator, using the average priced home in your market, what your commission will be and what her bonus will be for every referral she brings in.

I've ignored this in the past and have always felt it was a big mistake. This alone can be the difference between ordinary compensation and the chance for your new assistant to make really decent money. In addition, of course, if she brings in enough referrals, she will literally be paying for herself, which ultimately will have made hiring her a very good business decision.

Whatever you do, have the list turned in the second day, even if she needs to spend some time in the afternoon, on your nickel, working on it. My experience has been that this can slip through the cracks too easily and just never materialize. This is one of those things where *later* just never comes.

HANDS-ON TRAINING

For actual hands-on training, I recommend starting each task at its point of origin. In other words, use the first new listing you take after hiring your assistant as the pattern. Don't take an existing listing that's already been processed and explain how each step was done.

When you come into the office with a new listing, show your assistant where the appropriate file folder and check list are located, and walk her through the activation process. Show her how to put it into the MLS system and into your office system. The check list will be an excellent guide, and with the two of you actually doing the process together, she'll pick it up easily.

Go through this process with three actual new listings, then ask her to demonstrate her understanding and proficiency on the fourth.

NEW LISTING CHECK LIST

Seller's Name(s): _____

Property Address: _____ Price: _____

Home Phone: _____ Work Phone: _____

Listing Date: _____ Expiration Date: _____

Documents In File:

Listing Agreement: _____

Property Data Form: _____

Seller Disclosure: _____

Agency Agreement: _____

Lead Base Paint Disclosure: _____

Home Owners Association Contact: _____

Data Entered Into MLS: _____

Contracts Faxed To MLS: _____

Yard Sign Ordered: _____

Lock Box Code: _____

Photos On Web Site: _____

Virtual Tour Filming Scheduled: _____

Notes:
_____
_____
_____
_____
_____
_____

(Six Figure Income / Sue Christensen ©2002 All Rights Reserved)

Use the same process with teaching your assistant how to open and track an escrow. I was about to tell you that after over ten years of working with an assistant, I'm no longer a control monster and I'm perfectly comfortable with delegation.

The one exception, however, is that I still take the earnest money to the title company. It isn't a matter of trust, it's just that my signature on the contract indicates that the money has been entrusted to my care and it is in my possession. That's where I feel it should remain until I have a receipt to verify that it is now in the hands of the title company and the property is indeed, in escrow.

Again, use your check list, and begin your instruction to open the office file with the earnest money receipt. Provide the names and phone numbers of:

- Escrow officer
- Lender
- Cooperating agent
- Buyer
- Seller

Explain which party to the transaction is your client. Explain that each party has different responsibilities, and show her how the check list will be used to show her which side of the responsibility you're on for that particular transaction.

Again, work through three actual new escrows together before turning it over to your assistant on the fourth and watching for proof of proficiency.

ESCROW FILE CHECK LIST

Escrow Number: _____ Escrow Company: _____

Seller: _____ Buyer: _____

Listing Agent: _____ Co-Op Agent: _____

Lender: _____ Referral Agent: _____

_____ Earnest Deposit Receipt

_____ Requires Broker's Approval & File Number:

_____ Copy of Purchase Agreement

_____ Copy of Listing Agreement or MLS Data Sheet

_____ Copy of All Changes and Renewals

_____ MLS Detail Sheet

_____ Referral Form (If applicable) Tax ID#_____

_____ Escrow Instructions Complete With Signatures

_____ Final MLS Sold Change Order (If our Listing)

_____ Agency Relationship Disclosure

_____ Seller Disclosure With Signatures

_____ Buyer Inspection Notice And Seller's Response

_____ Lead Base Paint Disclosure (Built 1978 or prior)

_____ Walk Through Form, Signed

_____ Final Settlement Statement

_____ Termite Inspection

_____ Copies of Relevant Correspondence

_____ Other (Septic Certification, Well Inspection, etc.)

(Six Figure Income / Sue Christensen ©2002 All Rights Reserved)

Assistant Orientation Tips

You can spend the rest of your orientation time teaching your assistant the various other job responsibilities, such as:

- Follow up letters
- Contact management program
- Creation and placement of ads
- Handling in-coming calls
- Etc.

Be sure you stick close enough that first week so you can do whatever coaching is necessary with phone skills and greeting of clients.

At the end of the first week, spend the last thirty minutes on Friday reviewing:

- Ask you assistant how she felt about the week.
- Ask her what she liked best.
- Ask about any area where she needs more training.
- Tell her what you were most pleased with.
- Explain any area that you feel needs a little more work.
- Assure her you're planning to help her with this.

This is the right way to select, hire, and train your assistant. Done this way, you'll get off on the right foot and have a good chance of enjoying a long and mutually satisfying association.

Don't Make These Hiring Mistakes

Too often, we agents tend to:

- Hire in a hurry
- Train poorly
- Offer limited support
- Wonder why we can't keep anybody.

To do it right and make it a good business decision, we need to do more than:

- Hand our new assistant her office key
- Gesture to the file cabinets
- Show her the coffee and bathroom
- Throw a pile of check lists at her
- Turn her loose
- Expect her to function efficiently

Promise yourself that *just this once,* you'll commit to a careful selection process and invest the proper amount of time in training. Both will pay big dividends in the long run. Your office will run smoothly and efficiently, and you will be in a perfect position to *increase your production.*

Chapter Seven:
Systems For Everything

The next part of the equation is *Systems*. You need to have a system in place for everything that is done on a recurring basis. If you do something that works right once, set up a duplicatable system so you can do it again and again and ultimately, *lots* of times. We've already seen a few systems in earlier chapters, such as the system for setting up a new listing file and the system for tracking an escrow in progress. Essentially, the thing we're trying to do is avoid having recurring situations become emergencies by being unprepared. The purpose of systems is to make life easier and keep the stress level down as we move forward with the expectation of increased production.

The Prospecting System

We talked earlier about the importance of using scripts and dialogs. That's a system. Every salesperson of every product has a certain amount of call reluctance every day, so when you know *exactly* what you're going to say and exactly what questions need to be answered to gain the desired result, the reluctance is minimized if not entirely removed. With a familiar system, you're more likely to stay away from the old creative avoidance trap.

When you have a system for prospecting, you don't have to:

➤ Decide who you're going to call

➤ Look up their phone numbers

➤ Decide how you're going to keep track of results

➤ Figure out what you're going to say

All of those things are accounted for ahead of time in your system. All of these, left in an unprepared state, contribute to making us masters of creative avoidance. Throw in sharpening our pencils, getting a glass of water, and going to the bathroom a couple of times, and we've pretty well got it covered.

> ### THE PROSPECTING SYSTEM
>
> By contrast, here's what having a system looks like:
>
> - Prospecting is done at the same time every day.
> - It is scheduled as an unbreakable appointment
> - Our assistant has prepared our calling list
>
> We know ahead of time, from our contact management program whom to call:
>
> - Sphere of Influence
> - Past clients
> - FSBOs
> - Expireds
> - Just Listeds
> - Just Solds
> - ABC List

You may personally have selected the night before who you'll call from your ABC List, and possibly made selections from your Sphere of Influence list. Your assistant has prepared all of the other lists for you from your contact management program. If you're calling around a Just Listed or a Just Sold, that list has been prepared from your crisscross directory on CD ROM, of everybody on neighboring streets.

You have a call sheet you've designed that shows each category of calls, such as the one we saw in the chapter on prospecting. You have a written script for each category which you will use on every call, adding only the personal comments appropriate to the prospect's responses. Your two major questions are:

- "Where are you moving?"
- "When do you need to be there?"

You will make notes of each conversation that has potential, and a 'tick' mark of those that do not. Obviously, we don't want to waste time on those that have no potential for business, but remember we're getting in the habit of tracking our numbers, so we need to know how many calls we're completing irrespective of their potential value.

Your assistant will input the day's leads, with a next contact date, and enter the appointments you've made into your scheduler. This includes several systems within systems, but that's a general overview of the prospecting system.

THE FOLLOW UP SYSTEM

The follow-up system, obviously, relates to another contact in the form of:

- Another phone call
- A letter or personal note
- An in-person contact

All of these will be input into your computer and when your Call List is waiting for you on your desk every morning, that's where those names and phone numbers come from. While you were on the phone, you made some appointments in the high impact categories, such as:

- FSBOs
- Expireds
- Previously contacted potential clients

Having successfully made those appointments, you can't stop now and try to figure out what to take with you on those listing appointments.

There's already a system in place to make this very easy, and assure that you're always prepared. My system is color-coded so I can see at a glance whether I need:

- Red File Folder: for buyers (meaning *'hot prospects'*)
- Green Folder: for sellers (meaning *'pay days ahead'*)

When I get the appointment, I know which color file folder to grab, and I know it's already stuffed with all the necessary forms.

> **TITLE COMPANY FOLDER ITEMS**
>
> From the title company, I'll get:
>
> ➢ Legal description
>
> ➢ Assessor's Parcel Number
>
> ➢ Lot size
>
> ➢ Home size
>
> ➢ Year built
>
> ➢ Taxes

When I'm gathering this data, which only takes a few minutes, I vacillate, depending on market conditions, as to whether I want to know how much the Seller paid when they purchased. If you don't know, you could risk embarrassing yourself, but if you *do,* you may be influenced to establish a price that's not right. If you're absolutely sure you can make yourself be strong about right-pricing, it's probably better to know what you're walking into.

Then get the MLS data to figure the price. If they're upside down, they're upside down. The *market* is going to tell them that. You're just the messenger. Occasionally I've run into people who have come right out and said, *"Oh, I don't go by that." Everybody* thinks their house is worth more than it really is. Usually you can show them with factual market data, whether they go by that or not, what it's really worth. In the event you can't get their agreement with what you *know* is the right price, you have a decision to make. If they're way off the mark on their idea of value, and they're also attitudinally difficult (either a know-it-all, or belligerent), your decision is probably going to be that you don't want the listing.

Listen to your instincts, but don't walk away too soon. I've been paid on a lot of closed sales where the initial meeting suggested a very different outcome. Remember about going three deep. If you can see you're not getting anywhere on your recommended price, before walking away, here are two strategies you might use. Incidentally, both of these are systems, because:

➢ You've prepared ahead of time

➢ You've done it before

➢ You know what to say

Always assure them you want them to get every dollar they should, because of course *you* do. Then tell them about the appraiser's role in closing the sale, and that even if you *did* find somebody who would pay their price, you still have to stand up to the scrutiny of the appraisal process. Using a predetermined script say:

> "Mr. and Mrs. Seller, let me suggest this. I've already shown you in your net sheet that it's pretty common to split the cost of the appraisal with your Buyer, or even pay it yourself if that helps negotiate something else that's more important to you. If we're going to ask a fairly aggressive price, let's get an appraisal right now, and market very strongly that we're either at appraisal, or just below. If you'll do that, in the event there's any more expense related to appraisal in getting your sale closed, I'll guarantee you, in writing, that you won't have to pay it. Does that sound fair?"

What that means, you'll explain, is that if their eventual Buyer won't pay it, you *will*. Of course, they have to close with you, since you obviously won't be paying if somebody else has their listing at the time they close, and your written guarantee will say this. This won't really happen very often, no more than maybe three or four times a year tops, and at $125 per time to have the appraiser do an update, that's not out of line for three or four closings that earn you $5,000 each, minimally, on just the listing side, and would have earned you nothing if they had remained overpriced and didn't sell.

BUILT-IN PRICE REDUCTION STRATEGY

The other strategy I'm going to suggest in case you think you want to take the listing at their price, and believe they may realize their mistake later is this:

> "Okay, Mr. and Mrs. Seller, let's do this. Let's go ahead with your price right now, for two weeks. If we don't have sufficient showing activity by that time, to verify that people are taking us seriously, let's go with a price reduction. I have the form right here, and we can date it two weeks from today."

If you're using David Knox's video, *Pricing Your Home To Sell* in your pre-listing package (which we'll discuss in detail later), you won't get this kind of resistance much. They'll understand the impact of the first thirty days on the market, and if they're motivated, they won't want to screw up that opportunity.

BE STRONG ON PRICING

I cannot possibly over-emphasize the importance of being strong on pricing. Know your market and make the right tools, such as that video, available to your clients. You could buy as few as three copies of the video and use them in all your pre-listing packages, and pick them up when you're on the appointment. Tell them when you drop off the pre-listing package how important it is that they take a few minutes to look at it before your appointment. If you get there and they haven't looked at it, make it a part of your listing presentation and look at it *with* them.

I promise you, you'll have a lot fewer pricing arguments. Realize of course, that you won't get much business by arguing, so if you really want the listing, experience tells me you won't argue, but you'll take it over-priced, and that's when your troubles begin. Nobody will want to show it, no Buyer prospects will want to look at it, the Seller will be mad and you'll know it so you'll avoid them, then they'll be mad because they never hear from you.

Meanwhile, their mouth is running to everybody they know, some of whom are going to sell their homes next year. And while all this is going on, your expense meter is running, and your stress level is going up. It certainly does appear that it's a good idea to have a system in place for right pricing.

QUALIFY! QUALIFY! QUALIFY!

We've all heard the old adage that the three most important things in real estate are *location, location, location*. From our perspective as practitioners in the industry, it's *Qualify. Qualify. Qualify*. This applies to Sellers as well as Buyers, and I want to talk about it here, because a Seller's attitude about pricing will tell you a lot about their motivation, which obviously is *everything* regarding their qualification as someone we want to work with.

If you go through all of the above regarding right pricing, and they're still adamant about insisting on doing otherwise, I can just about guarantee you, the next thing that's coming is they're going to ask you to reduce *both* your commission and the length of the contract.

If you're just getting started, you'll do some of that because you need some listings, and you may not have the skill level quite yet to avoid it. We've all been there and done a certain amount of it, but I like it better now that that's not how I do it. As you know, commissions are strictly negotiable, and we'll get in big trouble if we say anything to suggest otherwise. So I'll just use myself as an example and tell you that in the residential market, I like 'six and six.' That's a six percent commission and a six month listing contract.

When I'm asked to go to five percent and ninety days, I explain that that doesn't work with my business, and I know from nearly twenty-five years of experience it doesn't bring them the motivated help they need to get what *they* want. The other agents need to see in the MLS system that they're going to be paid enough to make them move that home to the top of their 'Must Show' list. I, as their agent, need enough time to believe I'm going to get it sold before I'll be very comfortable spending my time and money to promote their home.

In the case of the color-photo magazine that most Sellers want to be in, the publication cycle is four weeks. If you list their home right when that magazine comes out, you have to wait another four weeks to get in it. That means if they want a shorter listing, they'll have to pay a *higher* commission, because you'll have to go to a more expensive form of advertising.

> **AVOID THE DEADLY THREE**
>
> I hope you won't *ever* cave in to what I call the 'deadly three':
>
> ➢ The over-priced listing
>
> ➢ A reduced listing period
>
> ➢ A reduced commission

The three simply do *not* go together, and the person who wants to combine all three in one listing contract absolutely does *not* qualify as a motivated Seller. Do everything you can to avoid this formula for disaster.

The easiest question to ask up front is *"when do you need to move?"* The answer to that question really needs to be a specific date; not necessarily August 14th at 8:00 am, but at least, *"Mid August."* If you get an answer such as *"We're in no hurry...Sometime next year..."* that type of thing, you can expect some resistance to the big three: price, listing period, and commission.

If you've done it right and spent sufficient time studying the scripts and dialogs and know which to use and when, you will have had this conversation on the phone when you were prospecting for listing appointments.

Far better to know early than late. If you've spent only a couple of minutes on the phone, and for whatever reason have not asked the key questions, and you still think it's a good house in a good area that you can sell, put the prospect on a *drip system.* Provide a little information in the mail at specific time intervals, and they'll become one of the calls you make regularly during your daily prospecting time.

You may establish a relationship that gets you the listing under desirable conditions that make it saleable. If you've called every twenty-five to thirty days and just said, *"Hi, it's Sue. I was just thinking about you. How's it going? Are you ready yet?"* You'll be the one they think about when they *are* ready.

By contrast, if you didn't qualify them right, didn't know there wasn't any motivation and they're just *thinking* of putting their home on the market rather than actually offering it for sale, you *will* run into the big three. Caught off guard, the odds are very high the conversation will take off in an argumentative direction, and the chances of your getting the listing will be destroyed. Be careful and know how to qualify. You must qualify *everybody* you're thinking of spending time with. It's your most valuable asset and it has to be spent wisely.

The Buyer Interview

Buyers will or will not qualify immediately as a direct result of your Buyer Interview, which is another important system. This is done on a specific form, and it's probably on red paper (so you'll know at a glance, which to pull out of your prepared forms supply), with the same questions asked each and every time you talk to a Buyer Prospect. The two most important questions are:

- *"When are you moving?"*

- *"What has to happen before you can move?"*

These answers may come up in your first phone conversation, so you may never have to actually ask. By the end of the conversation, you have to *know*, so pay attention, and do less talking than listening. You'll get your chance to talk later when it's *Show Time*.

If they call you, it's likely to be a sign call or an ad call, or perhaps a personal referral. They may begin by saying something like this:

> *"I'm in town from Cleveland, I just took a job at the hospital, and I have to be here in thirty days."*

You'll want to schedule them in immediately, since you know they're qualified relative to motivation. But you still need to determine that:

- They're financeable.

- There's nothing on the other end to prevent their purchase

When you've satisfied those two questions, invite them in for a Buyer Interview, which you're probably going to call an 'Initial Consultation' in conversation with them. With that completed, sign them up on a Buyer Brokerage Agreement, so you know they qualify to work with you, and you're set to find their dream house.

The Buyer Information sheet on the next page is used for the interview.

BUYER INFORMATION

Date: _____ Agent: _____

Buyer's Name(s) _____

Address:_____

Home #:_____ Office #:_____

Cell #:_____ Fax #:_____ E-Mail: _____

What prompted you to call?_____

What was it about the ad/home that you liked?_____

How long have you been looking for a home?_____

Are you working with another agent?_____ Who?_____

How many homes have you seen with other agents?_____

What kept you from purchasing?_____

Do you own or rent?_____ Must you sell before purchasing?_____

How soon do you need to move?_____

What needs to happen before you can move?_____

Have you arranged financing, or will this be a cash purchase?_____

Would you like to meet with one of our lenders while you're here?_____

If I commit 100% to you, will you commit to working exclusively with me?_____

Present Home: Future Home:

Price: $_____   Price:$_____

Bdr_____ # Baths _____   # Bdr _____ # Baths _____

Sq. Footage _____ Garage _____   Sq. Footage _____ Garage _____

We hope to duplicate (Features): _____   Our Top Wish List is: _____

_____   _____

_____   _____

(Six Figure Income / Sue Christensen ©2002 All Rights Reserved)

We do not want: _____   Must Haves Are: _____

_____   _____

_____   _____

Family Members;_____

Personal Interests:_____

Hobbies:_____

Notes:
_____
_____
_____
_____
_____

My signature below grants my permission to use family, interests, hobbies to introduce our family to our new neighborhood at closing. All other information is confidential.

_____   _____
Buyer   Date   Buyer   Date

(Six Figure Income / Sue Christensen ©2002 All Rights Reserved)

Six Figure Income

This basic form can be used for the initial qualification of any Buyer that comes to you in any situations. Obviously, not all questions will be used each time, as in the example of the people from Cleveland who are going to work at the hospital.

If you get a sign call, for example: *"Oh, I've just always loved that area. Can you show me the house at 9:30?"* Whoa! First of all, no, you can't show them the house at 9:30 because that's right in the middle of prospecting time, which you can't just blurt out to the caller; but just as important: can they really *buy* the house?

Always be kind. *Always.* Don't be tempted to say the old-fashioned and highly offensive *"I didn't get your name"* deal. You can get to that later. It's far more important right now to determine qualification. If it turns out they *are* qualified, their name will come automatically, without making yourself look like an *ordinary* salesperson and irritating them all in one step. This is better:

> *"That's a great area. Everybody's calling on that one. When do you need to move? Where do you live now? Oh, great. That's another nice area. Will you be selling your home to make the move? Oh, good for you, it's already sold..."*

See where this is going? Qualify, qualify, qualify. Then, of course, schedule a time to show *and sell* your listing.

What if the area they live in now and the house they called on represents a $300,000 price jump? Maybe it can be done, but that's *quite* a jump, and I think it signals the need for some financing questions. Again, be kind. How about this:

> *"Mrs. Buyer, when we look at the house, I want to make sure we have everything we need. I'll bring the MLS detail sheet, my own personal flyer with photos, neighborhood map and CC&Rs. Do we need any information on schools? Medical facilities? What about financing information, or do you have that arranged?"*

Since you only work from systems, you already have a lot of red buyer folders prepared ahead of time, and now all you have to do is add the personal stuff and you're ready for the prospect's arrival.

Safety Precautions

The prospect *always* comes to your office. *Always.* You do not meet people you don't know at the house. Period. Several years ago, I had a sign call on one of my listings (actually it was Larry and Arlene's house I told you about awhile back - the call I almost didn't make). The caller had been driving the neighborhood and wanted to see it. He told me it was for his son and daughter-in-law, who would be in graduate school and he'd be paying cash. He lived in

Phoenix and had a summer home in Forest Highlands. All of that told me he could, indeed, do pretty much anything he wanted to financially.

He definitely wanted that area near the University, and it was a *great* house, which I thought he'd like, so I was pretty excited. He asked me to meet him at the house, and I felt I should just be honest and admit that for safety reasons, I just don't do that. My theory was that honorable people would not take offense, and sure enough he said, *"I understand. I'll come to your office."*

When he got to my office, his wife was with him and I immediately felt very comfortable with both of them. This story, as you know, has a great ending. They bought the house, and we had a short escrow period. I was delighted when they came back and listed it with me when they were ready to sell. The point, obviously, is that having a system to preserve your safety will *not* cost you business.

Another time that same summer, I was asked to meet someone at a vacant house. You get a lot of that on sign calls, so it's important to anticipate this and be prepared, so you can get the appointment and the chance to make the sale, without risk of danger. My policy has always been to come straight out with it, rather than the old-fashioned *"Come to my office so we'll have everything we need."* That comes later; right now, we're just talking about the question of meeting someone you don't know alone at a vacant house.

This particular time, I told the guy that for safety reasons, I never meet anyone right at the house, and would he please come to my office. He said something about just being a block or two away, and he was in a hurry. He sounded okay, but a rule's a rule, and I think this is a serious issue that has to be followed to the letter.

Just then, my assistant came in, so I said, *"Okay. My assistant just got back from the post office, so I'll bring her with me,"* to which he shot back: *"Wait a minute. I'm alone. Who's going to protect me from you two wild women?"* laughing the whole time. Incidentally, he bought, too, so that's proof of my steadfast belief that honorable people are not offended by an honest admission that you're aware of the need for risk reduction.

Train your staff carefully and thoroughly in this area. Use common sense about sending anyone to a remote area to do anything: pick up a key, install a lock box, fill flyer boxes, deliver escrow papers, whatever. As you know, I'm a huge fan of outsourcing, and a real believer in having only one assistant, so we've developed systems that allow us to get good at doing as much as possible in the initial listing appointment. Photos are taken then, two keys are picked up so one can go in the lock box which is installed right then, etc.

But if you're going to provide superior service, and take extraordinary care of your clients, there will be times when somebody has to go to their home to do *something*. It may be to turn off lights that were accidentally left on, open all the blinds for a better showing, etc. Just exercise every precaution and have a real awareness of what's going on around you.

Talk about it in advance so your assistant and anyone else you bring in as contract help will know to be watchful and aware. As a matter of practice, I always lock the door behind me when I get inside, and I never answer the door at someone else's home. If I were approached outside the house and after getting out of my car, I'd have my little pepper spray companion in my pocket, or in my hand in plain sight. I've just always been pretty open about this sort of

Six Figure Income

thing, as in coming right out and telling people I'm not meeting them anywhere alone. We know from the earlier examples that honorable people understand the importance of such policies, and anyone else ought to be forewarned that you're not an easy target.

Another Look At Qualifying

In review: qualify all Sellers before you take their listing, and if they're motivated, move forward. Qualify all Buyers before you invest any time at all, other than just the Buyer Interview process. I'd spend as much as an hour on this, but *only* if they have satisfactorily answered the first two questions: when are you moving? what has to happen before you can make the move? Both of these will tell you if you have a motivated Buyer or a 'tire kicker.'

Frankly, I think we should qualify all the people from related industries who will interface with our clients in the closing process, to be sure they'll perform satisfactorily and in a timely manner.

Qualify Everyone Working With Your Client

This will include:

- Lenders
- Escrow officers
- Home inspectors
- Termite inspectors
- Appraisers
- Painters
- Carpet cleaners
- Etc.

The number one criteria I go by, aside from proper experience and strength of their company, is how quickly they return my calls. Never think you can get them to improve later. If you haven't had a return call from an affiliate within a couple of hours, and you know from experience with them or have heard they're great at whichever service they provide, you *might* try to call them again. But if they haven't returned your second call within an hour, move on to the next person on your list.

Yes, this is pretty hard-nosed, but here's the thing: *everything* that happens while the escrow is pending needs to run smoothly, or the client's perception is that they had a bad experience buying or selling their home. That comes back to rest with you, and can really affect future business. We need to look at this as much more than one transaction, and consider the lifetime value of each client.

Lifetime Value of A Satisfied Client

If every client you serve comes back for a repeat transaction and refers five other people to you conservatively, that part is easy to calculate by your average commission. Where it begins to compound exponentially is in the calculation of the repeat business of each of those five, and the five each of them refers. That's why it's critical to be absolutely sure that every other service provider recognizes your client as a VIP and treats them very well.

Life isn't a story book, and sometimes things will come up that will be less than perfect. My experience is that people can actually stand a fair amount of bad news, but they need to be told graciously, and above all, they need to know early, while there's still time to resolve it.

Yes, sometimes there are termites, and sometimes there are credit glitches, but people still move on with the sale, and people still buy homes every day. It just goes far better for you and your reputation if you make sure everybody who ever interfaces with the transaction takes it seriously, and takes very good care of those important clients.

Chapter Eight:
Putting Your Plan Into Action

Know Your Market

With a detailed business plan, based on goals which also must be in writing, and with some good systems, even if you're newly licensed, you can do business immediately. Somehow, you have to know a little something about your market. I'd recommend a personal visit with the humans behind the MLS computer, the staff, and director at your local association office.

Go and introduce yourself, prepared with a specific list of questions that will help you understand the number of homes changing hands on a monthly and annual basis in your market place and in each specific neighborhood. You will want to know:

> ### MLS Market Place Check List
>
> - Median price
> - Average price
> - Number of days on the market
> - Units sold in each price range
> - Size and features of homes selling
> - Age of homes selling
> - How does age affect market time
> - What are people buying?
> - Where are people buying?
> - Etc.

All of us humans love to be asked for our help; we love knowing that others respect our expertise. These people will be very happy to help you.

Then, early on, before you have tons of appointments, spend one hour a couple of times a week previewing homes. All of this is part of learning your market. Talk to appraisers to find out how certain factors influence value. Make careful notes and study them. Do this monthly so you're aware of changes in your market. I'd spend a couple of weeks, maybe a month right out of school doing this. If you've been at it awhile, but you want to jump-start your production, you may want to spend some time on this anyway, with a fresh new outlook on building your business to a new level.

You do have to be prospecting right away, so look for FSBOs and Expireds and get your ABC list together, so you can send out an announcement to at least a couple of hundred people. Then start calling five to ten of them each day, along with your other prospecting calls, to see if they know anyone who wants to move. When you've gotten a good start on all of this, look again at your business plan, checking the figures you used against the information you've gathered from your MLS staff.

Know the average sale price in your market. If it's $175,000 and you're new to the business, reduce it by $50,000, and assume that as a rookie, you'll sell some $125,000 homes. If the typical commission is 3% per side, calculate yours at 2.7%, so you've accounted for some 2.5% offerings in the MLS system. Always figure conservatively rather than set yourself up for disappointment.

Six Figure Income

With these two figures established, you know that the average commission paid to your office on your business will be $3,375. As a rookie, you'll probably be on a 60/40 split, with your Broker paying your expenses (except association dues and personal promotion). Sixty percent of $3,375 is $2,025 to you. How much money do you want to make? If you just left a $35,000 job, it's very common to want to go to the next bracket, so you might say $45,000. Actually two closings per month, or twenty-four units in your first full year is $48,600 in gross commissions to you. Clearly, none of us go from zero to six-figures in one leap, but following your plan diligently, you should be able to do it in two years.

Don't be tempted to speak of your production in *volume.* Not many people do that any more, and as we discussed earlier, a goal of a certain number of millions won't really tell you much that's useful. If you know you need to make two sales a month, or three sales, or whatever your goal and your plan tell you, in order to stay on track, that's a number that makes sense in every day real terms. It gives you a number you can relate to a lot of things as you get in the habit of working with your plan.

In the very earliest stages, you should only plan on about a twenty-five or thirty percent success ratio. If both of your closings are going to be from listings, you'll need to plan to go on eight listing appointments per month, or two per week. To be safe, you should schedule them at the front end of the week, so you have time to adjust and recover if you don't connect on one or both of them.

Fill The Front Of the Week First

Scheduling is your whole focus while you're prospecting, so make all of your calls with the idea of filling your earliest available Monday and Tuesday appointment slots first. Once they're filled, keep going and fill in as many time slots as you can. You have to allow for:

➢ Cancellations

➢ You decline due to over-pricing

➢ You and the seller aren't a good match

Frankly, at the rookie stage, you also have to allow for appointments with people who are interviewing more than one agent, and you just don't have the experience to be the successful presenter...yet. Try to schedule *a lot* of appointments early, so you get a lot of experience quickly, and be committed to learning from each and every presentation. If you do this faithfully, you'll soon have the experience you need to get very good, and you'll take a lot of listings.

Time For Action

That's where the fun starts and the action kicks in. You'll get sign calls and you'll be placing ads, so you'll get ad calls. Talk to your Broker and find out your office policy on sign and ad calls. Chances are, I'm afraid, that you'll find that both types of calls go to the floor person. That, as you know, is the person whose turn it is to take any potential walk-in or call-in business during their shift. Unless you can financially commit to paying an office bill, you may not be able to make much of a case for getting your own sign and ad calls. Your Broker may say, *"No, I paid for your ad and for your signs, therefore I say who gets the leads they generate."* Work hard and get strong quickly, because you need to be where you get all the leads your work effort is generating.

In all fairness, you really should be paying for your own ads if you expect to get the calls, and thus, the leads. Talk to your Broker with a completely open mind, focused on fairness. You may have an excellent enlightened Broker who will want to work with you on this. A Broker who sees your potential and wants to keep you happy so you'll stay can *still* only do what makes sense for the company. Ideally, maybe you can negotiate something between the floor person scenario, and the full blown hundred percent concept, where you pay *all* your own expenses, including a desk fee, and you get all your own leads.

If you had a Broker who typically paid new agents on a 60/40 split, and paid for fifteen column inches of advertising per listing, you might try to negotiate a 75/25 split and you pay for your own ads, *if* you could have the ad calls. In that case, you would put a direct number on a sign rider, and pay the cost of having the direct line installed as well as other related expenses, or use your cell phone. You might consider the Money Line that we discussed awhile back.

I'm sure you'll need to be prepared to assure your Broker that those calls will be answered promptly, so make your work schedule a part of your presentation when you approach the negotiations. Also, we've already established that you have an assistant, which is another means of assuring that you'll be made aware of all calls promptly, so you can respond immediately.

You'll shake up the non-producers in your office, but the good agents will respect you, and frankly, I think your Broker will *love* you. They can do the math, too, and they know anybody who is sharp enough to work from a business plan, and negotiate from a true business perspective, is going to be successful. They would rather have twenty-five percent of your income *and* your contribution to the company's market share, than have you tempted to go to a hundred percent office.

For a year or two, if you can negotiate anything this good, go for it. After that, as your average sale price and volume go up, you won't be able to afford to lose twenty-five percent of your income. You'll need to negotiate with your Broker again, this time with the expectation of paying a desk fee.

We're still talking about implementing your business plan, and we're working backward from the amount of money you want to earn, through the number of units it takes to get there. That's why your commission split, which determines your average commission, is critical to this discussion.

Chapter Nine:
The Pre-Listing Package and Listing Appointment

All change is challenging, but in order to change your production and your income, it is absolutely necessary to change your thinking process. That, of course, will change some of your daily work habits. The one thing that keeps coming up repeatedly chapter after chapter, relating to some phase of your business is prospecting. You simply *must* make prospecting a part of your daily life or nothing much is going to happen. We've explored several methods of prospecting, but the one I really believe has to be fully internalized and brought into habit as quickly as possible is that all important hour of telephone prospecting that's done first thing in the morning.

Once you get into the habit of calling the three critical groups:

- Your Sphere of Influence

- Your past clients

- Your ABC list

Those conversations will begin to feel as natural as calling any other friend, and people will come to expect your calls. Believe me, they'll respect you for it, and they *will* remember you when *"moving"* comes up in their conversations with others.

Set a goal to make a hundred contacts per week; that's all in person or by phone, not including any mailings. For our purposes right now, a 'contact' is a completed conversation someone who can make a buying or selling decision, or direct you to someone who they believe may need your services. It's not a message left on an answering machine, no matter how eloquent, or a message left with another person. It's a conversation with someone who gives you a direct answer to the questions:

> *"Who do you know that wants to buy or sell a home?"*

> *"Are you interested in selling your home?"*

Do not let your prospecting be influenced in any way by your ego. You *must* set it aside and get it out of the way. True, you may not sound perfect when you start, and true, some of your office mates, though not many, may tease you a little bit. Do not concern yourself with that. Let them feel foolish about prospecting, and let *them* stay at their $45,000 income. You're on your way to six figures. Believe in yourself and *do it*. Depending on your office climate, and the number of people who may fall into this category, you may want to do your calling from home, first thing in the morning, before you ever go near your office. Your assistant can fax your call list to your house. You also need thirty minutes a day for lead follow-up, and it could be that these calls are easier than regular prospecting calls. Perhaps you'll want to look at making your lead follow-up calls a warm up for your other prospecting.

Suit yourself, but I promise you, if you're on the phone every work day, talking to people about what you sell, you *will* sell a lot of it. If you don't do anything but this, write me and tell me about your success. I'm *positive* it will be there, and I love hearing about other people's successes. Many people try to avoid this, and they're the ones who, even after years in the business, are still trying to find the magic answer.

Another word of caution, make sure you're prospecting for *appointments,* not just *leads*. There was a time some years back, when the big thing was to have fifteen hundred or more names in the database, and frankly, I think that's just what they were: *names*. In truth, I doubt whether anybody really has that many hot leads, or even moderately workable leads.

You need to decide for yourself what's a 'lead.' I know many highly productive off-the-charts mega agents who don't consider anyone a lead if they're more than ten to fifteen days out from a buying or selling decision. I also know many people who will go only sixty to ninety days out, but candidly, I think a lot of business may be passed up by ignoring people who are as much as six months out. Remember, your assistant does most of the database management until the time to get them listed is pretty close.

I wouldn't want to see any good production time wasted on people who are just too far out from their decision, nor would I want you to fall into the trap of pretending people are prospects when, in fact, they are not. That happens when you prospect for leads rather than for appointments.

That's why it's important to practice, so you'll be good on the phone, then *get on it* so you'll become experienced as quickly as possible in being able to tell who is a prospect and who is not. In calling people with a known real estate need, you will definitely get appointments for Right Now business. In calling past clients, sphere of influence, and your ABC list, you'll get leads for Future business. You really need a good mix of both every day.

Your computer program will tell you every day who gets a letter, which letter it should be, and who needs a phone call. Your assistant manages this, providing you with a list every morning showing both, and later in the day, provides you with a stack of letters to sign. She then takes them to the post office for you, with a first class, commemorative stamp, please. Be noticed for quality, not confused for junk mail.

What's In A Pre-Listing Package?

Once you make the appointment, in most cases twenty-four to forty-eight hours later, do everything you can to make the prospect want to sign the contract when you get there. A pre-listing package is a great idea, because scheduling the appointment indicates that they have some inclination toward listing with you, and they just need some assurance that that's a good decision.

The Pre-Listing Package

Your pre-listing package includes:

- A copy of your daily schedule
- List of references and testimonials
- Sample marketing plan
- Profile of their property (from the title company)
- Specific marketing pieces
- Just Listed/Just Sold Cards
- Flyers
- Magazine ads
- Your personal brochure
- Copy of the contract they'll be asked to sign
- Copy of all other documents needed for listing
- Print out of your web site
- Seller's homework
- *Twelve Crucial Questions To Ask Your Agent*
- David Knox video, *Pricing Your Home To Sell*
- Microwave popcorn for viewing video

Add to this every snazzy marketing tool that shows you are the best agent they could hire. Also, use your digital camera and put photos of *their* home on the Just Listed/Just Sold cards and on the flyer. The psychological advantage here is *huge*. First, it shows you are prepared to begin marketing their home immediately. Second, in many cases it may confirm that you are *planning* to market it, therefore showing them that there's no need to interview anyone else.

TWELVE IMPORTANT QUESTIONS TO ASK YOUR AGENT

- What professional designations have you earned?
- How many years have you been in the business?
- How do you expand your real estate education?
- What is your average days on the market?
- What is your average list to sale price ratio?
- How do you communicate with your Sellers?
- Will you be marketing within my neighborhood?
- May I see a sample property brochure?
- What is your written marketing plan?
- May I see your resume?
- How many homes have you sold?
- How many homes have you sold in my area?

SHOW TIME: THE LISTING APPOINTMENT

The pre-listing package has been delivered, the prospects have reviewed it, and the hour of the appointment has arrived. It's *show time*. Nothing will ever beat the combination of *preparation and confidence*. From the instant you arrive, take charge. There is an art to doing this without appearing arrogant. If you truly care about people, you'll have some instinct for doing this, and experience will teach you the rest.

A cardinal rule you need to keep with you always in the sales arena is this:

Before you ever get what you want from anyone, you must first give them what they want from you.

In the listing scenario, what you need to give the Sellers from the instant you meet is:

➤ The absolute assurance that you know what you're doing

➤ Your sincere interest in the successful completion of their goal

➤ Assurance that you are *committed* to getting their home sold

I frankly think sometimes we agents can get a little arrogant in our belief that we are the busiest people in the world. The truth is, *everybody's* busy. Your Seller doesn't have time to listen to two or three lengthy listing presentations. That's partly the purpose of your pre-listing package: to reduce the time you spend on that listing appointment. It's intended to keep your schedule running well for maximum productivity, but it's also a matter of respect for the Seller's time.

Don't bore them to death with a lot of stuff they don't want to know. Talk about *them and their situation.* This isn't about you, it's about them. Your pre-listing package showed them all of your credentials as a great agent, and that's all that needs to be said about you.

In your first conversation you got the most crucial information: you qualified them for motivation to sell by asking them where they're moving and when they need to be there. Use this. Let them see early in the appointment that you paid attention and that you intend to help them get where they're going.

You also asked them some questions regarding their expectations of their agent. I assume that you're prepared to do what they said they want, and that if their expectations had been incompatible with the services you offer, you would never have scheduled the appointment. I am also assuming that you determined from your phone conversation that they are somebody you want to work with relative to their attitude, as well as their motivation.

My advice is, rely on your pre-listing package to have shown them what you do to get properties sold. Walk through the house and then go straight to your market analysis so you can establish value. Bring out your contracts, which are filled out except price, and place them in plain sight, where the Sellers can see that you came expecting to list their home right then and there. I know many people who do a lot more business than I do, who go in with everything filled in, including price. That's their system and it obviously works for them. This is mine, and my belief is that I've shown enough confidence to have the contract all ready for

SELLER'S INFORMATION

Have you supplied us with: Two Keys _____ Seasonal Photos _____

Your Lender: _____ Loan #: _____

Here are things we think are great about our neighborhood:
_____
_____

Here are things about our home we think a Buyer would like to know:
_____
_____

Information about our neighbors: (ages & number of children in area, etc.)
_____
_____

What we've liked most about this home:
_____
_____

Other thoughts we'd like to share:
_____
_____
_____

Seller's friends, fans, and family (Minimum 50; Christmas Card List is ideal)

Please send a Flyer about our home to the following:

Name	Address	Phone

(Six Figure Income / Sue Christensen ©2002 All Rights Reserved)

signatures, but I understand that it's *their* home, and they deserve the respect of *actively participating* in the pricing decision.

Do not start the pricing conversation without asking if they've watched the David Knox video, *Pricing Your Home To Sell*. If they haven't, watch it with them now. This will eliminate 99% of the pricing questions and objections. It's *that* strong.

Be Prepared To Walk Away

What if they *still* want to list at an outlandish price that you know will cause the property not to sell? Discuss it, show them the market analysis' factual information, have the *"Let's get an appraisal"* conversation we talked about earlier. Be prepared to turn it down if they won't be reasonable.

The most useful thing I've heard for this tough situation came from my favorite CRS instructor, Del Bain: *"I'd rather **turn** you down now, than **let** you down later."* Wow! That's powerful. We know that people begin to make plans and decisions based on what we tell them we believe we can do for them, so it is enormously important to be responsible in pricing.

Sometimes people will know how strong you are in the marketplace, and will be completely taken aback that you might not accept their listing. Then they may say, *"But we really want to list with you."* Going three deep, you'll ask again for your recommended price, and in situations like this it's very common that they may say they *"just want to try it."* Your response will be: *"Based on today's market conditions, I'm afraid I simply cannot help you at that price."* At that point, they'll either sign the contract, or you'll respectfully thank them for their time, wish them well and *leave*.

Throughout this entire conversation, which has probably taken no more than thirty minutes from your arrival, you have been the consummate professional, and have undoubtedly made a high quality impression. Oh, they'll find somebody who will take the listing at their inflated, unsaleable price, but when it expires and you call *immediately;* they'll remember your class and integrity, and you'll get the listing then...at the right price.

Let's look at the realistic, highly motivated Seller, the one who accepts your advice from the beginning and signs up right then, Be prepared to do as much as possible right at the listing appointment, and be prepared to make sure you don't disappoint them. Do what you say you're going to do. It's always better to *under-promise* and *over-deliver*.

Have your digital camera with you and take the publicity photos right then. Show the Sellers what's going to be used and how, and be prepared to download the photos into your MLS system and your web site that same day. Don't tell the Sellers they'll be viewed world-wide that day unless you're absolutely sure they will. The minute you tell them, they're going to call great aunt Harriet in Cincinnati, and they'd better be there.

If you find out that either system has hit a glitch, call your Sellers immediately and tell them. Don't let them find out for themselves, or they'll think you *already* fell short of what you promised. It'll be hard to recover completely.

Instead, tell them what you're doing on your end, and that presenting the photos to the world at large is now an MLS issue, or a web host issue, and that you'll let them know when they can go online and see for themselves. Project a specific and realistic time line, then make sure your assistant calls, and as always, the procedure is: *"Sue wanted you to know right away..."*

Remember to pick up the video and the completed Seller's Home Work. Their answers in the questionnaire may have something unexpected that may be really helpful for your ads, and it's possible they may have a friend who is interested in the area, who will show up on the list they're providing for sending out flyers.

Much of the information you've had on file from your earliest conversation was recorded on the Listing Information sheet, which is shown on the next page.

LISTING INFORMATION

Date:_____ Agent: _____

Seller Name(s): _____

Property Address:_____

Home Phone #_____ Office #_____ Fax #_____

1. Where are you moving?

2. When do you need to be there?

3. Do you own any other properties?

4. Are you interested in selling them too?

5. Has your property been on the market before?

6. When?

7. Was it listed? With Whom?

8. How did you hear about us?

9. Are you interviewing anyone else?

10. What are you looking for in your agent?

11. Do you need help with an agent where you're moving?

12. When would you like to meet? I have _____ open, or would _____ be better?

Notes:
_____
_____
_____
_____
_____
_____
_____

(Six Figure Income / Sue Christensen ©2002 All Rights Reserved)

Section IV:
Making Yourself Famous

Chapter Ten:
Providing Legendary Service

In all cases, you'll want your Sellers to receive a Thank You right away the next day after you've taken the listing. A handwritten, personal Thank You note is always a good idea; again, in this age of technology and automation, it's out of the ordinary. An excellent way to *plus* this and make an extra strong impact is to send the note to their work place attached to a rose or carnation in a bud vase delivered by a florist. This expresses your sincere appreciation for their business and it says you're somebody who cares enough to pay attention to details.

All their co-workers will want to know who sent the flower, and a common reaction will be, *"Wow! What class. What a nice thing to do."* The unspoken thought will be *"My agent never did anything like that for me."* What if your Seller is a couple? Send one to each of them and double the impact.

Later when you get a contract and it's been fully negotiated, you'll send a note of congratulations in exactly the same way. Likewise, a third note and bud vase will be delivered when their Buyer's loan is approved, removing the final contingency.

A fourth and final delivery will be made on closing day, but this time it will be a bouquet of helium balloons which will make a very festive splashy statement of celebration. Project how many transactions you plan to do in the next twelve months, then make a deal with a nearby florist, close enough that your assistant can easily and conveniently run by with your handwritten note to accompany each delivery. You'll get a great price, probably about $5 for the bud vases and $15 for the balloons. Even if you have couples, you're looking at probably $60 per listing to make an incredible splash.

> **SPECIALLY DELIVERED THANK YOUS**
>
> The deliveries are made to celebrate:
>
> - The Thank You for the listing
> - Congratulations on a successful purchase contract
> - Congratulations on approval of the buyers' loan
> - Congratulations on the successful closing

Your clients will love it and think you're the greatest person in the world, but far beyond that, look at the impression you're creating in their work places. Their co-workers who saw this will remember you as somebody who really goes the extra mile when they get ready to sell their homes. They'll also tell others, so it's actually a relatively inexpensive courtesy that will return exponential dividends. Another benefit is that of being well received later when you contact people in those businesses to ask if they know anybody who is thinking of buying or selling.

I used to be concerned about what to do if they don't want anybody to know. Don't worry about it. If they feel this way, you'll know right away because they won't want a yard sign. In that case you won't take the listing, because you and I both know *you can't sell a secret.*

Memorable Housewarming Gifts

Take your housewarming gift over to the house on the day of closing. I've done several things over the years, but the ones I've enjoyed giving the most, and that have brought the best feed-back are:

- Trees for new construction purchases
- Crystal vases for couples
- Museum memberships for families with children

In the case of new construction, you can't choose somebody else's landscaping, but I have yet to meet anybody who didn't enjoy receiving a flowering crab apple tree. The thing I love most about this, besides knowing that in a small way I'm helping beautify the world, is the feed-back. It's fun running into people around town and hearing them say, *"We were just talking about you last week when we realized how much your tree has grown."* Over the years, I've had a lot of variations on that theme and each one tells me those folks see that gift as a connectedness that is special.

The crystal vases are very dear to my heart, because when I deliver them, always beautifully gift wrapped with a handwritten note, I usually tell the man I had the notion that he was probably the type who is always bringing home flowers. You can't believe the calls I get from women who tell me that even if he *wasn't* the type, he is now. Look for things like that that will really pay dividends *for your people,* not for you. Although I have admitted that I am truly a flaming entrepreneur, I am against any kind of housewarming gift that has your name on it, or any other kind of commercial look or feel to it. Far better, in my humble but correct opinion, to plant a seed for something that the clients can pick up and run with to their own eternal joy. They will remember you without your having done anything so obnoxiously self-serving.

As you know, I have absolutely no qualms about waging a totally shameless self-promotion campaign, but this is neither the time nor the place to do it. Let the spirit of caring and gratitude guide you when it's time to say *"thank you,"* and let the spotlight be on the new home owners.

STAYING IN TOUCH

You'll have your chance to remind them what a great agent you are and how well you served them when you get into your follow-up program. If your Seller has stayed in the area, chances are you probably sold them another house or connected them with the contractor who built their new house. In both cases, you want to stay in touch with them by letter at:

- One month
- Three months
- Six months
- Nine months
- Special one year anniversary card

Then you go to once a year, on the anniversary of their closing, remembering that they're in your database as past clients, and they're contacted quarterly by phone when you're prospecting for referral business.

This kind of caring and special treatment is the thing that makes people feel they have a friend in the business. Your name will come up in conversation with their friends who want to move, along with, *"Why don't I call her for you?"*

Obviously, the whole idea is to have a lot of this type of relationship-based referrals to help build your business. It's also where the deepest personal satisfaction lies, in having a number of people who respect and admire the caring and integrity with which you served them. This comes only from your unwavering commitment to the clients whose trust you have earned through serving well.

Uncommon Courtesies

Several chapters back, I mentioned the extraordinary work ethic of my friend, 'Sarah,' whom I worked with for many years in Vermillion. She probably did more than anyone I've ever known in the area of customer service. I learned many things from her in those early years of my career, but none more important than this.

Sarah did things for her clients that were unthinkable to the competitors who envied her seventy-five percent market share. I went to work with Sarah in July of 1978 and within the first week I got a bird's eye view of the amazing work effort that went into that phenomenal domination of the market.

That part of the upper midwest is a very seasonal market due to the harsh winter climate, and is further defined by the University's school-year calendar. Virtually all of year's sales are made from May to September, or at least they were at that time, with the heaviest activity in July and August.

I joined Sarah right at the height of the summer frenzy of activity. Daylight Savings Time made it possible to show property as late as eight or nine o'clock at night, write contracts until ten or so and then do whatever else we had to do to keep up, even later than that.

Within the first week of our working together, I became aware that one of the homes that was closing the next day had just been vacated; Sarah was going to run by and see if it had been cleaned. I offered to go with her, and to make a long story short, she and I were there until after midnight cleaning it ourselves.

You may recall that Vermillion is a very small town, so there were no formal cleaning services. We still cleaned our own homes at the time, so we had no idea who to call, even if we could have gotten anybody on such short notice.

The lesson to me, however, was that Sarah never complained or did any fussing about the condition of the house. The people were long gone and that would have been pointless. She simply had a standard for the condition of any house she turned over to her Buyers, and was prepared to do whatever it took to make that happen.

An even more valuable lesson came the next day. Right at the end of the closing at the bank, Sarah excused herself to go out to her car to retrieve the one last key that we'd *"accidentally forgotten when we cleaned the house last night."*

She hit that *so light* that the focus was on the *key*, not the cleaning, yet the Buyers picked up immediately on exactly who had made it possible for them to move into a clean house.

I've never known anybody in all these years who had a higher rate of repeat and referral business, but of course, I've never known anybody else who went to such lengths to provide that level of service.

Another thing that was unique to that market, or at least vastly different from Arizona, is that all the houses had basements - finished basements - and in the spring and summer, those basements had water. Not all the houses, obviously, and not every summer, but often enough that we had to deal with the problem.

In what was probably the rainiest summer on record, we had an unusually high percentage of listings where the Sellers had already vacated and moved away before having their homes sold and closed. While other agents were calling their Sellers to inform them of *their* problem, we were having sump pumps installed and *resolving* the problem.

For several years when we were faced with that situation, our husbands and our collective four sons used shop vacs to extract water from carpeting, detached the carpeting, hauled it up the steps to dry in the sun on the driveway. We then installed sump pumps and returned the carpeting to the rescued family rooms, which we'd dried out with big fans. Whew!

All of us had our regular jobs and the boys were all in school, so during the flooding crisis, the basement rescue mission all happened at night and on weekends. Now *that* is customer service, and I've always been grateful to have learned it early in my career.

It's nice to live in a large enough town now, where most any service needed can be hired rather than wrestling with such emergencies personally. Always, a very high standard of care should prevail, and in the event that something catastrophic should occur, obviously, the right thing to do is simply whatever it takes.

CLIENT APPRECIATION EVENTS

As your business grows and you can afford to do more, think seriously about some kind of client appreciation party. When you've served people well and have done your follow-up right, accepting your invitation will be the most natural thing in the world. I don't necessarily recommend actually *calling* it a 'client appreciation party.' I think you go much farther by just having a 4th of July Party or maybe at the holidays 'adopt' a needy family, and make it a festive occasion to get a group of friends (who happen to be clients) together to help assemble gifts and food for them. As your business grows, adopt several families and keep inviting the same great people every year, always adding new client-friends. Your invitation might say something like this:

You're Invited!

Our clients are the greatest people in the world. Let's all get together in the spirit of the holidays, and share our good fortune with some families who really need us.

Please come by our office Saturday, December 8th from 10:00 A.M. to 12:00 Noon for Lattes, Cocoa, and Christmas Cookies.

We'll have Santa on hand to talk to your children, and we'll have some elves handy to help. Assemble any toys and non-perishable food items you'd like to contribute to the families we'll 'adopt' as a group.

During the party, invite help with the gift wrapping and delivery and make both of these very festive. Serve *very* light refreshments and don't worry about their simplicity; the focus is on the *camaraderie* not the usual party trappings. Have your most photographically-talented friend taking a lot of pictures if you can't afford a real photographer. If you can, that's one place where it's really worth it to splurge. Of course, you've designed a very nice folder to frame the photos, then you sign them and send them to *everyone* along with your thank you note.

Say Thank You With A Photo

There are many different ways you can go with this:

- Individual photos of the kids with Santa
- Entire families with Santa
- Groups of friends with or without Santa
- Photos of people wrapping gifts
- Photos of people assembling food baskets
- Photos of people making deliveries

If you put any of these photos in your newsletter, send copies to everyone in the pictures, as well as sending the individually framed photos.

> **MORE IDEAS FOR CLIENT APPRECIATION EVENTS**
>
> Other ideas that are nice client appreciation/celebration of friendship events are:
>
> - Easter Egg Hunts
> - Ice Cream Socials
> - Halloween parties
>
> Be very clear in your invitation whether the event is to be:
>
> - For the entire family
> - Adults only

In all three of these, you really would do well to include the entire family, and have special activities for each age group you expect. As a general hint, teen-agers won't usually attend, but be prepared with a current-release movie just in case.

Younger kids will really get into various activities at an Easter Egg Hunt, and will love finding the treasures you've hidden for them ahead of time. Be very careful to let the different age groups do their hunting in waves that do not overlap. If at all possible it would really be good if separate areas of the park, or of your own yard if you have the room, could differentiate the place for each age group. If space does not allow, go with the youngest group first and progress through the various age groups at timed intervals to be sure each child enjoys the success of finding some eggs. As each group awaits their turn, they are having their pictures taken with the Easter Bunny, and of course, these will be framed and sent to the participants with a thank you for attending.

At an Ice Cream Social, you'll probably need some commercially-made supplies if the group is sizeable; otherwise, round up several freezers and do home-made ice cream. Everybody loves it and the novelty makes it really festive. Have several toppings and an assortment of sprinkles, chopped nuts, etc. You could easily get a lot of help with the refreshments if you're comfortable telling your guests in the invitation that they're welcome to bring a dozen of their favorite bars or cookies. The best way to encourage them to participate is to ask them to bring the recipe to be compiled in a special cookie book.

I'm really big on things like this so you have something to send as a follow-up. In my opinion, photos of the participants themselves and booklets of *their* recipes are things that are likely to be kept and valued.

> **EVEN MORE IDEAS FOR CLIENT APPRECIATION EVENTS**
>
> A family Halloween party is another great idea, which can be centered around:
>
> ➢ The guests' costumes.
>
> ➢ Carving or painting jack o' lanterns
>
> ➢ Ghost stories: open mike style

All of these will make great subjects for photographs again, for your newsletter, and as souvenirs to be sent to your guests. Always, the photos have the year and the event on the folder/frame. These are nice reminders of happy times you all shared.

Another thing that is great fun at the holidays is an old-fashioned Cookie Exchange. This you may want to do with several smaller groups, rather than having everybody at the same time. I like groups of ten at a time, because that tends to require only two batches of cookies to be made by each participant. Be *very clear* on your instructions. Some people are unfamiliar with the specifics on how a cookie exchange works. I've done tons of these, and with the first couple, I guess I wasn't clear enough, and you wouldn't believe how shaken a couple of my guests became.

The first time, I guess I hadn't made it clear that it was necessary to bring ten dozen cookies of one kind, individually packaged so one dozen could be given to each of ten people. The whole object, obviously, is that you end up with a wonderful assortment of cookies for the holidays, and you only had to bake once. Well, this first year, one lady showed up with fabulous cookies, but they were all together in one huge tin, and she was mortified to discover that everyone else's were individually packaged.

Another year, I guess I hadn't emphasized strongly enough that they were supposed to be *fancy* Christmas cookies. One of my guests was pretty steamed because she had fussed for God-knows-how-many hours putting frosting Santa faces and beards on cut-out sugar cookies and someone else had just brought regular chocolate chip cookies. You never know when someone is going to view something so non-life-threatening as *that* serious. Just try to be clear in your invitation so such incidents can be minimized. Also, be sure to ask everyone to bring a few extras to sample at the party. Again, a recipe book is a nice follow-up thank you.

These, by the way, can be produced in-house for very little money, and can be sized so they fit in a nice envelope for easy mailing. Be sure to work it into your invitation that part of the value is that you only have to bake once - two batches of your favorite holiday recipe-and you take home a lovely assortment of cookies for your own holiday enjoyment.

One of the best ideas I've ever seen for bringing clients and friends together came from a friend in Austin, Texas, who has elevated wine and cheese on Sunday evening to an art form. He does these parties in his home about every six weeks. He has a core group of friends he invites every time, and mixes in clients, ending up with a rotating group of about twenty-five each time. He provides the cheeses and other snacks, but he invites the guests to bring a bottle of their favorite wine to share. I think he's wise to do this, because then it doesn't become so cost prohibitive that he's forced to do it less frequently. He always has some type of mixer activity or game, because he's a Buyer Specialist, and most of his clients are new to the area. This is just a great way to help them meet other people. He pays very careful attention to everybody's conversational comments while they're working with him, and uses these details to put together people with similar interests or another common thread.

The first few years we were in Flagstaff, I did a Newcomers' Club which was somewhat similar. It was a lunch at a different restaurant each month with just the ladies, and it was a Dutch-treat situation. It went very well and the ladies seemed to enjoy the opportunity to meet others and make new friends. We included the men quarterly for dinner, which again was 'no host,' at various restaurants, and we even went dancing once. When your group becomes too big for restaurants is when you'll want to take a look at a holiday event or a summer picnic at a park.

STILL MORE IDEAS FOR CLIENT APPRECIATION EVENTS

Other things that people will enjoy will depend on what's available in your area. If you have snow, have a Winter Carnival where everybody can get involved in:

- Making snowmen
- Making snow angels
- Making snow castles
- Sledding
- Ice skating
- Toboggan races
- Snowshoe races

Cocoa and roasting marshmallows for s'mores are real naturals for snow events. Again, watch for those photo ops and send them to everybody.

If you live near a beach, that's another great opportunity for a summer party. You'll want to provide the hot dogs and watermelons, but it's perfectly alright to pot luck the salads, deserts, etc. You'll probably want your guests to bring their own beverages, other than soft drinks, to move the liability away from you. You may want to think about hiring a clown for photos with everybody, especially the kids, and line up some activities such as face-painting, balloon artistry, and games.

After awhile, when you've had your groups together several times and there are multiple over-lapping friendships, you'll be gratified to find that people are taking the initiative to expand those friendships individually.

All of these things we've just discussed are two-fold. On a personal basis, it's *always* good manners to say *"thank you."* From a business perspective, we're discussing a very thorough system of building your repeat and referral business. Conventional wisdom does have a point that high-volume producers do the greatest percentage of their business with listings, but the fact is *Buyers* are more likely to stay in the area and send you referrals. This is the biggest reason I've always felt it was important to have a good mix of both Buyers and Sellers, but here's the key:

Relocation Buyers are the ones most likely to take a tremendous amount of time, and have a greater tendency to pull you off your schedule. The Buyers you want to work with are repeat clients and personal referrals.

Within the first five minutes of meeting a new referral client, you'll want to acknowledge the person who sent them to you, and assure them you're going to do everything you can to make their real estate dreams come true. Then conduct the Buyer Interview just as you would with any other Buyer. During that process, you will make the determination from their comments what needs to be done to help them realize their goals.

Have your new client fill out the usual questionnaire that will give you detailed information as to who they are as individuals:

- Their hobbies
- Special interests
- Perhaps even a secret passion

This will give you the ability to send magazine articles and small gifts from time to time when you see something that reminds you of them, as your relationship builds.

I have another real estate friend who loves to send *Chicken Soup For The Soul* stories to various clients and friends on a regular basis. All of these little things, the out-of-the-ordinary special personal kindnesses you can extend to people will enrich their lives and make *you* more memorable.

Following Up The Easy Way

The best long-term follow-up program I'm aware of is Dave Beson's *Letter Writer* program, and it's available in software, so it's an automated system that's easy to use. It helps you stay in touch with your clients for seven years, and Dave is just a master at the composition of these very well done letters. Don't waste time reinventing the wheel when he's already done it for us. Even more important, don't leave it to chance and get too busy to actually follow through with your good intentions.

Chapter Eleven:
Personal Promotion

Standing Out in The Crowd

The organizations you're actively involved in are another great source, and while you're interacting with fellow members, there are a number of things you can do to make yourself, and what you do, noticeable. If you regularly attend meetings of thirty people, you're all going to know each other personally. If you just go to see two or three of these people each business day, in exactly the same manner you 'door knock' your ABC List, you'll easily get through the entire membership every couple of months.

When you're with this group of friends, learn to pay close attention to details in conversation. You'll pick up on people who have a penchant for investments and you may be able to help them acquire some income properties. Somebody else may like the idea of living in the country, but currently they're in town in a regular subdivision. Maybe somebody else is ready for a townhouse so they can eliminate yard work. There are clues all around us all the time, and I call picking up on them tuning in your real estate antenna.

There are subtle things you can do that will *invite* real estate conversation. I'm not real big on name badges, but I love real estate jewelry: just regular old costume jewelry, and there's a lot of it available now; it's eye-catching and it does invite comment. RE/MAX has done a lot with the hot air balloon in pins, pendants, earrings, tie-tacs, etc. Century 21 has some nice pieces with their logo, and all the other major franchises have created things that make people connect you to real estate when they get used to seeing you wearing it.

Get some polos, T-shirts, jackets, sweaters, etc. with your company's logo. If you're with an independent, have some things made. Granted, some logos may be catchier than others, but the whole idea is to train people you see often to make the solid connection that will make them think 'real estate' when they see you. Then they'll remember you whenever real estate comes up in conversation with anyone.

This can work with people you don't know as well. Wear logo items everywhere you go, and without your saying a word, even people you don't know will know you're in the real estate business. You'll find that when you're in line at the post office, at the supermarket, waiting at the polls to vote, etc. people will bring up real estate related conversation. They'll comment on current interest rates, seeing a lot of signs around town, property values, etc. Then it's perfectly natural for you to ask them about *their* home: where they live, how long have they owned their home, etc. If you know your market well, you'll be able to pick up on whether or not they might be a candidate for making a move. At the very least, you can ask if they know anybody in their neighborhood who may want to move.

Depending on how it goes, you may want to hand them your card, and perhaps get their name and phone number for future follow-up. Then put them in your database, and of course, follow up the same day with a handwritten note about how you enjoyed talking with them. It'll make a great impact, because you've shown your interest in them in response to a conversation *they* initiated, rather than calling them out of the blue at an inopportune time like all the rest of the telemarketers.

My favorite story about real estate jewelry is a Chamber of Commerce story. I've been an active Chamber Ambassador for years, and one of the best things we've sponsored are monthly New Member lunches. Those are typically attended by thirty to fifty people, including the new members, Chamber staff, and the Ambassadors. One day a few years back, my assistant handed me a note and said, *"Here's a call you're going to want to return right away."* A lady had gone into the phone book, looked up our office, called in and said she'd just attended a Chamber lunch and met a lady who was wearing a bright rhinestone hot air balloon pin. She'd met so many people at the lunch, she couldn't keep all the names straight, but she remembered the pin. That's exactly the way it's supposed to work.

I've noticed at conventions, that many of the vendors have generic pins that would work for any company. I have a little 'gold' house with a For Sale sign and Sold rider, and a couple of different styles of rhinestone sign post pins that just say 'Sold.' For men, there are similar things in tie tacs, lapel pins, and tie clasps.

As I mentioned, don't let being with an independent stop you. Have some things made that will work for you. There's an independent office here in town that's a perfect example. The couple who own it did it right and had their logo professionally designed with artwork that is perfect for Northern Arizona, and it's probably the classiest and most distinctive logo in town. Their entire organization wear logo clothes all the time. It's made them highly recognizable and their company is only a few years old.

Developing a Theme for Your Promotion Campaign

The official part of your actual personal promotion campaign is literally, everything you do to promote yourself, and should have a central theme. One of the best exercises I've ever seen to generate ideas for a personal promotion came from my favorite CRS instructor, Del Bain, in a class he taught in Albuquerque a few years back. This would work really great as an activity for a sales meeting, if you're so inclined, but most ideally, for your Master Mind Group. Remember that if you don't have an official Master Mind Group yet, whoever you regularly brainstorm with is your group, and this would work fine in that context as well.

Each person tells the group what their hobby is, then you go around the circle and everybody takes turns throwing out ideas relating to the hobby, while the person receiving the collective ideas writes them down for their own future development. One of my hobbies is music. I love collecting and listening to CD's by a huge assortment of artists and music types. Some of the ideas the group suggested for me were:

- In Tune With Your Real Estate Needs
- In Perfect Harmony
- She's Singing Your Song
- Your Perfect Theme Song
- The Melody of Your Dreams
- Conducting Perfect Moves
- Always Upbeat To Serve You
- Tuned In To Your Needs
- Leader Of The Band
- All Sharps...No Flats
- Never A Sour Note

The one I loved the most and ultimately actually used for a fun and effective campaign was *"Orchestrating Perfect Moves Since 1977."* I rented a traditional black tuxedo with a white pleated shirt, red bow tie, and red cummerbund, and had a series of photos taken at a local studio. The photo for *"Orchestrating Perfect Moves"* was a full body shot with a conductor's baton, posed as if to strike up the orchestra. The most fun use of that photo, and the one that's brought the most comments, was for an ad in the Flagstaff Symphony program.

At the time of the photography session, I had a head and shoulders shot taken that I've used on my business card, personal brochure, web site, and various ads. Another fun spin on this: I had some pictures taken with me in the tux, with a top hat, and a magician's wand to use with the slogan, *"Some say she works magic!"*

This type of thing can all be in circulation at the same time, because the common theme of the tuxedo photos ties it all together. For over eleven years, my tag line has been *"Sue Christensen Sells Flagstaff,"* and I've never changed that. But for certain specific ads, you can do some pretty creative things, such as the *"Orchestrating Perfect Moves"* idea that I've used for the symphony program.

That was just a black and white vertical business card sized ad, and it appeared in every issue of their program for the three seasons I used it. That's not necessarily the type of thing where you can directly trace a specific number of listings or sales, but I've had a lot of favorable comments about it, and it's the kind of promotion that contributes to the perception of *"we see you all over the place."*

I recommend having new professional photos taken every two or three years, because of hair style changes, etc. When I have the next set done, I'll do the tuxedo theme again because it's so unique. The orchestra conductor and the magician idea, and using the head and shoulders shot have been very effective for me, most likely because the uniqueness of the tuxedo theme is very distinctive.

The creative energy that comes out in a session like we had with our CRS class is amazing. I highly recommend you do it with your group. One of the reasons it's good to do it outside of your marketplace is because people are so much more willing to share and open up with great ideas if you're not all in direct competition with one another.

Who do you regularly see at conventions, seminars, and area sales rallies? Get out the cards you've collected at these events and pick out five or six people you liked from a break-out session, networking events, or anything else you noted that was a common thread between you. Choose people who live within a driveable distance from a central point, and create your own group if you haven't already done so. The Flagstaff, Phoenix, Tucson triangle worked very well for the group my friends and I put together, so I'd suggest something of that nature.

Let Your Imagination Go Wild!

Just use the Master Mind Group to compile a number of theme ideas related to your hobby. Then on your own, when you have plenty of time to think about it, let yourself go and imagine photography ideas that would make great promotion pieces.

Uses For Your Promotional Theme

Think in terms of using your most creative ideas for:

- Business cards
- Brochures
- Magazine ads
- Specialty ads
- Mailing pieces
- Billboards (if your area allows them)

Think about all of these uses, and anything else you can visualize that will make you stand out and be noticed in your marketplace. Then figure out the most effective attention-getting and attractively photographed outfits you want to wear, and take everything, along with a list of poses you want to take, to your photography session. Be sure to keep an open mind and listen for ideas from your photographer. Most people in that field are highly creative and may offer the best idea of all.

Blow Your Own Horn

Look for high-profile events where you can participate, wearing the same outfit as your photo, where you'll be seen by a lot of people. If your community has a business expo, home show, or something of that nature where you can set up a booth, have your picture enlarged to poster size for the back-drop, and be there meeting the attendees wearing the same outfit they'll see in the picture. This is very effective, because you are then the live personification of the photo they'll take with them on the hand-outs you distribute.

Always have a drawing for something that ties in with your theme. The whole point of your drawing is to track how many people visited your booth, to add to your contact base, and also to make it fun for the people who attend, which will definitely increase your traffic. In the case of the tuxedo with the *"Orchestrating Perfect Moves"* theme, a great drawing idea would be a year's membership to the symphony concerts. The corresponding group in your town will love it because they're always glad for the additional support, and people will flock to the booth because it's usually considered a pretty big deal to hold those season tickets.

In the case of the top hat and magic wand thing, tickets for a Lance Burton magic show in Las Vegas would be a great prize, and it would work here because it's a short easy drive or a very inexpensive flight to get there. What a great tie-in for the *"Some Say She Works Magic"* theme.

In both cases, you'll incorporate a lot of beautiful photos of homes you've sold, along with glowing testimonials from your happy, satisfied clients, with a creative presentation piece such as sheet music for the orchestra theme, and maybe beautiful homes being magically pulled out of a hat for the magician theme.

The follow-up correspondence you send to everybody who entered your drawing carries the same theme. Before long, people will begin to think of you in connection with your campaign theme. You'll start encountering situations where you'll meet someone you don't even know, in out of context places, and *they'll* strike up a conversation with *you*. *"You're the lady who . . ."* or *"I saw you at . . ."*

I've always stuck pretty close to the belief that for every disadvantage we have in working a small market (most notably, reduced numbers of homes selling and prospects buying), we have at least one advantage. Never is that advantage more apparent or more strongly felt than in the area of personal promotion. It is much easier to become a recognizable figure in a small market. Having said that, if you live in a large metro area, you can certainly become recognizable in one particular area, even if its population is fairly significant. Do what is memorable, and above all else, be *consistent*.

Using Your Theme For Mailings

For mailings such as newsletters, you must show up in your audience's mail box at least monthly, and no, you can't skip a month now and then. It must be monthly and it needs to carry a continuation of your theme. The consistent use of a common thread each and every time is the rule, which is where your creative photography comes in.

Consistency In Mailings

If you use a professionally produced newsletter, even though the news changes, the consistent common thread is:

- Your photo
- Your logo
- Your tag line
- Your contact information

In other words, the common thread is your face and your return address. Make them memorable. Unless your letter is *known* to carry some piece of information that people value and look forward to, they're throwing it away with all the rest of the junk mail. So make sure you look good *and memorable* on your way to the trash.

The key to establishing a readership is putting something inside that they'll want, such as the neighborhood market data insert I told you about that I use in my newsletter. This really is the basis for nearly all my 'Come List Me' calls, and I love providing that one piece of information the people find useful and interesting. I never kid myself into believing they're dazzled with the brilliance of the newsletter itself. However, this same audience sees all of your other publicly circulated promotion pieces, which is why having everything tied to a central theme is so important. All of those name impressions and theme impressions help strengthen one another, and make you memorable when the time does come that they need your services.

I tried recipe post cards one year, alternating every-other-month with the newsletter, but I found them to be less effective. They were a beautiful, high quality, full color piece, also professionally done, but the feed-back I got was that the newsletter was more appreciated. In truth, of course, it was the insert people really wanted.

SIX FIGURE INCOME 133

WHAT'S IN A NAME?

If your name is 'Baker' or 'Cook,' by all means do something massively creative with recipe post cards. There are some really great ones out there, and they're a good value for the money. But get the enlarged, over-sized cards that are two to a regular sized sheet, so you have room for the neighborhood market data on the back.

Then, once a year, maybe at the holidays or the beginning of the year, send a special folder to hold all of the cards, with an offer to 'cook up' a special marketing plan for those who are making a move this year. Use a theme that ties in with *"Old-fashioned Goodness,"* or *"Down Home Comfort,"* or something with 'taste' or 'flavor' that connects their home, cooking, or baking with your interest in them as people.

If you use Just Listed and Just Sold cards, or Meet Your New Neighbor cards, these can all tie back in to the professional photography gold mine that came out of your Master Mind Group brainstorming session relating to hobbies.

Don't substitute these for your newsletter, but be aware that when they're used along with a newsletter, people are seeing the same photos of you all the time, which are now becoming recognizable. These are all service-oriented pieces when they carry the right message.

One of my favorite phrases, which as far as I know I coined myself well over twenty years ago, is *"I just wanted to extend the courtesy of . . ."* In the case of a Just Listed card, use it like this:

> *"I just wanted to extend the courtesy of letting the neighbors know first, that 123 Elm Street is available for sale, in case you have a friend who has expressed an interest in your area."*

People appreciate things like that. If they do know someone who loves their area, maybe it will be useful to them at the right time. But the real idea is to cement in their mind at every possible opportunity that you are their neighborhood expert.

In the case of a Just Sold card, use it like this:

> *"I just wanted to extend the courtesy of letting you know, the house at 123 Elm Street sold for $250,000 in eighteen days. If you know anyone else who wants to sell, please feel free to pass on this card so they can call me. I've kept the names of everyone who looked at that home and may want to see others in your area."*

That verbage *may* get you a few Come List Me calls, but again, its purpose is to reaffirm that *you are it* in their area. Done frequently enough over a period of time, you may end up with people you don't even know passing your cards to friends because they think *you are it* all over town.

Meet Your Neighbor cards are great because everybody wants to know who's moving in.

Remember the questionnaire from the Buyer Interview that tells you who the family members are, ages of kids, pets, hobbies, etc.? And remember that we had them sign it acknowledging that we planned to use it to introduce them to their new neighborhood? Now we're set. This type of card builds a tremendous amount of good will, and this particular system also helps with risk reduction.

Keep all of these on file for use in future promotional activities, and for a quick refresher course when you get ready to do a client appreciation event. You may want to do a Neighborhood Services Directory sometime for things such as baby sitting, lawn care, snow removal, pet walking, house sitting, etc. If you do that, I'd recommend that you not have commercial businesses, and do this strictly as a courtesy for kids who do this kind of work.

SYNCHRONIZE YOUR PROMOTION CAMPAGAIN

You're well on you way to a pretty strong personal promotion campaign if you have, with the photos illustrating the same central theme:

- A newsletter
- A series of special-use postcards
- Flyers in the boxes on your yard signs
- The signs themselves
- A series of well placed ads
- Participation in high-profile events

Make sure you keep your photo updated and current so you'll be recognized when you do have the opportunity to participate in community events. Also, when you're just out and about doing normal activities, you want to be recognized.

That starts to happen a lot after about the third or fourth year. You will have some recognition *much earlier* but it comes in small doses at first, so hang in there and keep going with your campaign, always focusing on consistency and never losing sight of the big picture.

At about that third or fourth year, a lot of people will begin to recognize you and speak to you on the street as if they *know* you. That's why you're doing all this: people feel more comfortable doing business with someone they know. In the case of a big purchase or selling something with as big an emotional attachment as their home, besides feeling like they know you, they want to feel sure you know what you're doing. *There* is the value of the *"we see you all over the place"* (and have for a long time) perception.

BE SEEN EVERYWHERE

Here are some more ideas to make it look like you're *everywhere* at a reasonable cost. Whether you're in a small market, or working a specific area of a large multi-suburb area, look for all the small-town-type promotional opportunities. Who has a newsletter or publication you can get in for not much money?

I've been in our local Country Club's newsletter for about eight or nine years for $33 a month, and in the Chamber of Commerce newsletter for $50 a month since its inception five years ago. The Country Club is only a business card sized ad, and the Chamber newsletter is a quarter-page of a regular sized sheet. Both are just black and white ads, and circulated to the membership of both organizations. But here's the best part: now that everybody is into the internet, small ads can be very effective.

> ### KEYS TO AN EFFECTIVE AD
>
> All you really need in your ads is:
>
> ➣ Your theme photo
>
> ➣ Your company name
>
> ➣ Phone number
>
> ➣ Web site

Everything we do should be driving people to our web sites, rather than spending ourselves broke on elaborate full-color ads. I'd rather have a small ad in everything in town than one big snazzy ad in just one place.

I still do a full page ad of color photos of homes in the most popular magazine in town, because so far, both Buyers and Sellers seem to value that. I'm thinking that soon I will be able to take that to a half-page with a few Feature Homes, and encourage people to go to my web site for more homes and highly detailed information. It seems logical to me that people who are in from out of town may not necessarily have a laptop with them, so I'll continue to provide at least some *specific homes* information for them, and a presence for myself in the marketplace.

Truly, the best advertising you can have is a lot of your signs all over town, in front of homes for sale, and I think your signs should have your photo on them.

> **'PHOTOGENIC' SALES**
>
> My theory is, put your photo on all of your promotion pieces:
>
> - Your business card
> - Your web site
> - Your personal brochure
> - Your yard signs
> - Your own newsletter
> - Magazine ads
> - Other people's newsletters
> - Event programs

You'll be seen by a lot of people and you'll start getting comments like, *"Wow! I see you all over town. Business must be good."* That's precisely what they're supposed to think. The whole idea is, the next time they think 'real estate,' you want them to think, *"Let's call her. She must be doing things right to be all over town."*

When you're putting your personal promotion campaign together, do it for a full year at a time. Two years is even better. Use a lot of different media, as many as you can afford and will make good business sense, but before you start anything, look for all the high visibility opportunities in your town. Every town has them. Some of the obvious ones besides the two newsletters already mentioned are sponsorship-related.

TAKING SPONSORSHIPS TO A NEW LEVEL

Flagstaff has a Winter Festival because we're the biggest town in Arizona with snowfall, where people from the warmer parts of the state and immediate area can come for winter fun. There are programs to put ads in, a really cute parade with the charm and community pride only a small town can offer. I'm sure your town has something on this order. You could show up at such events as a spectator, wearing a logo sweatshirt or jacket, handing out theme-related flyers of a small gift such as candy canes at the holiday parade or little flags at the 4th of July parade, and attract huge attention without spending much money. Tie whatever you do in with a common easily recognized theme, probably your logo, and you'll make a great high-visibility splash.

Does your town have a good Little League program? Most towns do, and they're all looking for team sponsors. About $300 will put your name and logo on the T-shirt of every child on *your* team. You may want to take this a step farther and have T-shirts made for the parents with *"My Little Leaguer is on Jane Smith's Team."*

Find out when the kids play and show up with your private label bottled water for kids and parents alike, and with your magnetic car signs, that have the same logo as:

- The T-shirts

- The bottled water

- All the ads they see regularly

Bring your moving truck if you have one, and use it to hand out the bottled water. Could you do anything similar to help a school team or group? There's a lot to be said for having your name and logo turn up in a few dozen households' laundry a couple of times a week.

Still, the season does end, so what about taking a team picture and giving it to each child, framed in a decent but light-weight cardboard folder with your team name and the year. Nobody ever throws that kind of stuff away. Depending on how well it goes, even if your team doesn't win the league, I think it would be nice to sponsor a family picnic in celebration of the season. You might not have to provide much more than the hot dogs and soft drinks, with the parents bringing pot luck contributions.

Kids should, in my opinion, be rewarded for being good kids, and I think it's nice to look beyond just the initial sponsorship for ways to make the experience extra special for them. They'll remember you, and if they do, their parents will. All of this combined probably won't cost much more than $500 or $600, and you will have made quite an impact on the participating families. Plus, you'll have the attention of all the other team families whose sponsors just provided T-shirts. Probably most of the other sponsors are engaged in other business besides real estate, and you may be remembered by a family from another team when they get ready to move.

Another thing that our Chamber of Commerce does that's very cost effective is a Mid-Month Mailer, a packet of flyers that goes out to the entire membership. In Flagstaff, that's over a thousand members who can be reminded of your expertise for only $100 plus the thousand flyers you provide. If you're set up to produce flyers in-house, that's a very inexpensive way to add to your *"Wow! You're everywhere"* campaign. See if your Chamber does something similar, and if they don't already, maybe you could volunteer to help get it started.

While you're at it, get on a committee. The Chamber can use the help, and that'll give you another networking group. I was on the Chamber Board of Directors for six years, and simultaneously was a very active Chamber Ambassador. That turned out to be a lot of fun, it helped our Chamber with a number of projects, and I did a tremendous amount of business with fellow volunteers. Many of the people I served with in the Ambassadors and related committee work ended up becoming some of our best personal friends, which was a great bonus.

One of the best agents in our market place, 'Glenna,' who has a very successful office, does a weekly column on helpful real estate information for our local newspaper. Does your community have a similar opportunity? Contact your local paper or a magazine and ask if they'd like you to contribute something of this nature. You can write it yourself, or you can subscribe to a service that will do your column for you, so you're never at risk of running out of time as your deadline approaches.

In this and all of your other personal promotion, always do your homework. Watch what's going on in your area and be sure you're not stealing anyone else's thunder or stepping on anyone's toes. I'm not referring to harnessing what should be fair competition between professionals, What I mean is you probably don't want to find out after you've handed out 500 little flags at the 4th of July parade, that the League of Women Voters has been doing this as a sponsorship fund raiser for years. If you're always careful about doing your homework ahead of time, you'll receive full benefit of the promotion without having anything back-fire on you.

Giving Something Back

I'm still looking for ways to help our local non-profit organizations. I know many agents in other states who donate a percentage of their commissions for every referral they get from the non-profits, but the state of Arizona will not allow that exact form of donation. We are prohibited from payment to non-licensed entities or individuals, as I suspect most other states are. I'm sure there's a way to do it, but I would want to be absolutely in strict compliance with all of the legalities and regulations of the State Department of Real Estate. Clearly, anybody can donate to any charity whenever they wish, and I do as much of it as I can, but here, such donations cannot be a percentage of a commission.

If you have successfully implemented a program of this type that does comply with all of the laws and regulations, please email me and tell me about it. I will be forever in your debt. In our business, we do have to promote ourselves, obviously, so why not do it where it can help others. There is so much good that could potentially be done to help, that I'd really like to set up a good program to do this.

Giving back is tremendously important whenever and however we can. Less than one percent of the United States population ever earn a six-figure income, and when we reach that level and go well beyond it, we all need to do as much as we can to help others in the community where we do business.

Chapter Twelve:
Implementing Ideas

Sorting and Prioritizing

We've said before that it's important to get around people who are doing more than we are doing. In part, this is because we need the exposure to higher levels of production and better ways of doing things for inspiration when we need to raise the bar, and so we can always be finding ways to improve our business and improve our lives. One of the great ways to do this is to attend the conferences, training events, and conventions that I have referred to as the 'national events.'

Somebody suggested years ago, and I wish I could remember who so I could give them credit, that we should choose the top four or five ideas that could be implemented immediately, at the end of each day of a conference. Assuming it's a three or four day conference, we will end up with somewhere between twelve and twenty great ideas.

Then when you get home, the first thing to do that's very important is: *do not take any appointments or go near your office.* Spend that first day back - the first full day, not your travel day - reviewing your notes, paying special attention to those top twelve to twenty ideas. From this list, choose your top twelve, one idea which can be implemented each month over the next year, and assign each a priority. By doing this, instead of just jumping right back into business as usual, you will devise a plan for implementation, rather than having a lot of great ideas you never get around to using.

Some of the ideas, maybe even the majority, will relate to marketing, so you'll probably have a great start on your next year's marketing campaign. Naturally, you already have some things in place that you're really happy with and that are working so well you'll want to retain them. The Top Ideas list will undoubtedly show you a number of new things you'll want to add.

The next step is to figure out the time and expense related to preparation for each one. This will also help you in deciding which to do first, and which will come later, and precisely when that will be.

Remember to always do your marketing plan by the year, and resist the temptation to arbitrarily add something that isn't planned just because a good salesperson showed up with something that seemed like a good idea. They're almost all good ideas, so if you react and get pulled off track each time one is presented, your marketing plan will have no continuity and no direction. It will really be just a series of panic promotions, and will not be as predictable and measurable as necessary in order to build a successful long-term business.

Back to the top twelve ideas: the whole point of implementing ideas this way is so each one will have had a chance to become comfortable to you with a few weeks' use before another is added. Building in multiple ideas all at once holds the potential for having none of them really get off the ground. I've made every mistake there is in this regard, and spent a fair amount of time and money that ended up being wasted, all with the best of intentions, but without the proper amount of thought to a systematic plan of implementation.

THE TOP TWELVE SYSTEM

I always come home from the big national events just bursting with excitement about all the great things I want to do. This is great, but I'm glad I've learned the Top Twelve System and used it over the years. It has proved to be:

- Much more manageable
- Much more cost effective
- Much more sustainable

Having determined your Top Twelve, go through your notes again, this time looking for great ideas that can be implemented:

- Without spending any money
- Have no learning curve
- Have a minimal learning curve

Some of the most valuable ideas you'll pick up from others will fall into this category. Some will be a small but highly effective thing:

- An addition to your in-coming call log
- New method of qualifying leads
- Dynamite phrase to add to a phone script
- Great phrase to add to a standard letter

A lot of these things would be at risk of getting lost as you progress back into the real world of doing business and attending to the myriad related details. That's why it's really important to take off the entire first day back and go through this process of sorting and prioritizing.

This time through your notes, you're not looking for major ideas that will become a part of your marketing plan, or anything as big as a special event or a stand-alone promotion. You're looking for the little gems that will help you continue to get better, and you'll find that most of them relate to customer service.

In other words, the first time through your notes, you'll probably find that most of the ideas that hit your list will be in the category of attracting new customers. The second will relate more to keeping them: making them happy with your service and making them want to send you referrals.

THE LARGER-THAN-LIFE THINGS

BECOME A STAND OUT

Now go through your Top Twelve a third time, and let this be sort of a dreaming session. Look at the new ideas you saw that turned out to be:

- The biggest
- The grandest
- The most spectacular

This time, you're looking for things that will make you *really* stand out, and will make you special, unique, and memorable in your market place, such as:

- A courtesy moving van
- A VW 'Bug'
- A PT Cruiser
- A Humvee

These are all useful as vehicles, but from a marketing standpoint, obviously, they are also 'rolling billboards.' They have professionally done graphics and photos of you, and your logo, along with your slogan, and your phone number in numbers as big as they can make them. The courtesy moving van to lend to clients who buy or sell a home with you is a major attention getter. In recent years, the other vehicles have become increasingly popular among top producers, and are Mini Billboards which can be enormously successful in drawing attention to you.

The things in this category are obviously the big ticket items, much more expensive than the first two lists you made from your conference notes and hand-outs. They're the ones that require the in-depth scrutiny of: How much does this cost? How effective will it be? How does it relate to my gross commissions total? For an agent who wants to do thirty to forty transactions a year, grossing $150,000 to $200,000, this may make less sense than somebody with a goal of seventy to a hundred transactions grossing $300,000 to $500,000. *Be careful here.*

MAKE DECISIONS THAT FIT THE BIG PICTURE

Can you spend less money effectively and get noticed in your market place enough to get in the $150,000 to $200,000 bracket? Yes, you can. Can you get noticed enough to do two or three times that? Maybe, maybe not. The critical thing here is to analyze. One person with one assistant, with an effective marketing plan, great systems in place, and a serious committed prospecting habit can very comfortably do $150,000 to $200,000 in business and have a very pleasant manageable life.

Taking the quantum leap to double or triple that, you probably have to:

- Add staff

- Add a big attention getter

- Consider a balance of both

When considering these options, look carefully, and if you do decide to do something that will dramatically increase your business, don't do it all at once. You may find that it could cost less than you think for the big moving van if you can find a leasing company that will:

- Do the graphics

- Coordinate the specialized liability insurance

- Lease the vehicle, all in one payment

This rolling billboard needs to be out and be *seen* all the time. Your assistant can coordinate the schedule for your clients to use it for moving into their new homes, and to keep it parked at high-visibility locations around town when not in use. You also want to remember that the whole point of having it, besides offering a customer service that no one else has, is so it can be seen wherever there are a lot of people.

SIX FIGURE INCOME
143

Some of the obvious high-visibility uses are:

➢ As a parade entry

➢ Lending it to local charities

It can be used almost like a float in the 4th of July and holiday parades in your community. You can also get huge mileage out of it by lending it to local charities for their events. If an organization needs to transport a lot of stuff anywhere:

➢ For an event

➢ To set up at a park

➢ At the fairgrounds

➢ At the community center

You'll be their hero if you offer to lend them your van, and a lot of people will see it as your billboard when they attend the event.

LETTING THEM KNOW

Also look at the people you'll reach when you contact all the non-profits and fraternal organizations in your town and let them know you're willing to lend them your van. Here's how you do that:

➢ Send a flyer with a picture of the truck

➢ Theirs to use on an availability basis

➢ How to make a reservation

➢ Any other procedural requirements

Laminate the flyer and ask them to put it on their bulletin board. Laminating will cause them to perceive the flyer as something of value and hang on to it, posting it where you'll then have a mini-billboard at their headquarters where it will be seen frequently by everybody that's involved with their organization.

Food Drive/Holiday Toy Collection

Another great way to use it is for a holiday food and toy drive to help those in need, with this procedure:

- Park it in front of your office
- People can come by to add their donations
- Personal invitations to your clients
- Advertising to encourage public participation
- Do it on a Saturday morning
- Very simple refreshments and coffee
- Have Santa there

Ask people to bring their kids and let them mail their letters to Santa. Have a special decorated mail box for this purpose. Anything of this type that includes kids will improve attendance, and look at the good you'll be helping your group collectively do for people who really need it. Another thing that will dramatically increase participation is to invite a local radio station to do a live remote.

If you're more interested in one of the smaller vehicles, see if there's a way to make one of the cars part of an employee compensation package. Whoever does your errands and deliveries and gets around town a lot should be driving it. It, too, can be parked wherever it's going to be seen by a lot of people as a rolling billboard.

You will want to retain ownership or the leasehold interest, but most people who do errands and deliveries as a part of their job will appreciate the use of the vehicle during the business week. You can work out a plan where they:

- Pick up the car Monday morning
- Leave it at the office Friday night
- Have someone fill flyer boxes Saturday
- Move it to high traffic locations Sunday

Somebody in your office will have teenagers who will be glad to help move it around on the weekend for a small fee. You may even want to hire that same youngster to make the rounds filling the flyer boxes, in the cute car of course, which will take care of two things at once.

Another great attention getter that costs way less money and will help you in many ways with visibility, is purchasing a tent with your graphics all over it which is also made available for use by non-profits and fraternal organizations. It is less useful on a daily basis than the moving van or the cute little car, but in a climate where it can be used almost year-round, it would still be pretty effective. If your climate is seasonal, chances are your town probably has the majority of its major events during spring and summer and maybe even into the fall, when you could make good use of your tent. Your accountant will be able to help you assign a value to your donation of the use of the tent to help make it even more cost effective. In that sense, it could come close to eliminating the cost to you.

Zero-Based Advertising

I love zero-based advertising. In its true form, that's a type of advertising where the cost is shared by sponsors. I once did a Professional Services Directory, which was a simple, but useful directory, professionally printed on a single sheet of high quality, heavy glossy stock, which when folded once, became a four page piece the size of a regular standard sheet of paper.

The front and back had my graphics and photo and were all about my real estate services, and the two inside pages were business card ads for sixteen businesses that homeowners would find useful. Each participating business paid $250, which is nothing for a full year's advertising, and that covered the cost of printing 10,000 directories. Each participating business was given 500 directories for distribution to their clients and customers.

I kept 2,000 and included them in every pre-listing package and relocation kit I sent out. I also sent them to my entire mailing list. They were useful in many ways. If a soon-to-be-listed property was in need of some sprucing up it offered my clients direct access and generally some sort of a preferred customer discount for:

- A handyman
- A painter
- A landscaper
- A carpet cleaner

That was definitely an *everybody wins* situation that helped bring new business to several other small businesses, and of course it's paid off more than ten-fold in the referrals that have come back to me. It is also a nice way to introduce the businesses to newcomers to town who are looking for those types of services. The actual time invested was minimal, and the cost to me was literally zero.

Another zero-based marketing piece I did a couple of years ago was the production of a multimedia presentation on CD ROM for referral business. It was targeted to other real estate agents out of our area. I took it to two big national conventions and distributed it at literally *no cost* by putting one on each chair at the opening general session of both.

The presentation showed a lot of beautiful pictures of Flagstaff, describing what a well-located, scenic, and great place it is to live, along with a lot of detail about:

- Climate

- Major Employers

- Education Opportunities

- Medical Facilities

- Cultural Offerings

- Recreational Opportunities

It also told about my partner and me, our qualifications, track record, and real estate experience.

This was all done professionally by a company specializing in this sort of promotion and it was done right when this sort of thing became available, so it was expensive. The total cost for production, graphics, sound, and photography was $18,000. We had four sponsors to share the cost:

- A lender

- A title company

- An insurance agency

- A building contractor

Each of them paid $2,500 to advertise their business, which left my partner and me each paying $4,000. That was quite a bit for us for one marketing piece, but we recovered our cost and a small profit from the first two referrals. Of course, we've been very loyal to those four business friends whose participation made it possible, and we've sent them a ton of referral business. Zero-based advertising, when it works the way it's supposed to, is great for all who participate.

Section V:
The Realities of Life Balance

Chapter Thirteen:
The Big Picture: Keeping All The Balls In The Air

Now you've cultivated the two critical habits of script practice and prospecting, partly for Right Now and Future business, and partly for referral business. You've learned the importance of scheduling and implementing systems. You've hired an assistant, set up a good computer system, and you've mastered delegation.

We've talked about marketing and personal promotion, and we've talked about the pre-listing process and the results-driven listing presentation. We've reviewed the Buyer Interview, we understand the importance of qualifying, and we know about the critical element of follow-up on all of these things.

We know that all follow-up must be focused on the client, and that we must bring a serving heart to the equation along with superior business skills. These skills can be learned from a number of sources including:

- The great trainers I've mentioned repeatedly
- This book
- Software programs
- Other reference materials
- Books and tapes

The serving heart element will really be present in an evolving state as your experience level progresses and from a desire to be guided by the principle of *doing the right thing*. In other words, by being truly focused on the needs of your client and keeping their best interests at heart. If you're in it just for the money, success will elude you, but if you're guided by a desire to serve with integrity, the rewards - both financial and personal - will follow.

Yes, I have admitted to being a flaming entrepreneur, and I am well aware that there are easier ways to save the world. That's not what I'm talking about here. I'm talking about the attitude and mindset of truly *serving* your clients. This is what builds long-term relationships, and it's what builds the referral-based business that will bring you long range success and enormous personal satisfaction.

In sales, nothing ever feels as good as having a client return or send you someone they care about. It's their way of saying, *"I felt so well-treated that I want the experience again,"* or *"I want my friend to have the same great experience."*

Nobody who's doing a whirlwind, carbon copy, let's-get-this-over-with-quick business will ever experience this at the same level as you will when you *know* you did what was right for the client. This isn't anything that will ever come up in conversation it's just a matter of principle that's always with you.

It's a kind of faith in the goodness of serving well for the right reasons. It's when this principle supercedes everything else, that you'll receive your highest rewards. It's worth repeating: *always* do the right thing and the money *will* follow.

DELEGATION RE-VISITED

When you've reached this point in your career, it's time to take another look at delegation. We've already delegated a lot of the logistics of dealing with Buyers by referring many of them to our colleagues. Remember how easy that was?

Just make the decision that you'll take only repeat clients and personal referrals and take no relocation Buyers. These are the ones who take so much time that they will prevent you from sticking to your schedule and building a solid business.

Here's a real world example of fitting it all together: On say, Tuesday, October 24th, you have a Seller who wants to list her property, and a Buyer in town who is relocating with the hospital and wants to be in escrow by time his plane leaves on Sunday. You also have tickets to a Neil Diamond concert in Phoenix at 8:00 that evening that you bought in June, and you're going with your husband. What are you going to do?

That's an easy decision for me. I'm taking the listing appointment at 1:00 in the afternoon so I don't disrupt anything to which I'm so fiercely committed in the morning. I'll be back to my office by 2:30 with the signed listing contract, which I'm going to hand to my assistant, and I'll delegate all the steps to be taken to activate that listing.

> **DELEGATION AT THE OFFICE**
>
> ➤ In-putting it into the MLS system
>
> ➤ In-putting it into our office system
>
> ➤ Downloading the photos from the digital camera
>
> ➤ Ordering sign installation
>
> ➤ Creating a flyer
>
> ➤ Creating the Just Listed Cards
>
> ➤ Mailing the Thank You note I prepared ahead
>
> ➤ Checking our database for buyer matches

I'll refer the relocation Buyer to one of my colleagues for a 25% referral fee. Since it's a $500,000 purchase for the in-coming physician, my colleague is elated to have the chance to work with such a high quality Buyer. She's more than happy to pay me the $3,750 referral fee. In this process, relating back to having systems in place, *everybody* in this scenario is happy, because they all got what they wanted.

The Seller of the new listing is thrilled because she got all that immediate attention, and is left with no doubt that she listed with someone who is intensely interested in her and her goal. The Buyer got connected with a great, experienced agent who will make every minute he has in town count to the fullest, and make sure his needs will be met with great care and attention. The colleague you referred or delegated the Buyer to thinks you're terrific because this is probably the biggest sale she's going to make this year. Your assistant is happy because she has interesting, meaningful work to do. She also feels good about helping the new Seller, and about the respect and confidence you've placed in her. Your husband is happy because, without missing a beat, you handled everything and didn't even *consider* derailing the long-made plans for some private personal time. You're happy because you helped everybody else get what they wanted and needed, you did a great job of continuing to build your business, and you're off to have a great time with your husband. Probably even Neil Diamond is happy because you're coming to his concert.

Did anybody who contacted you to enlist your help as the best real estate agent in town even *know* that you had plans? Did they know that everything that happened that day had to be worked *around* those plans? Absolutely not. A true professional always makes the client feel that they alone are the most important person on the planet at that particular time, and that is a true pleasure to have the opportunity to serve them.

The referral form on the next page is used to delegate Buyers.

Preferred Client Referral Form

Referring Agent: _____ Date: _____

Referred To: _____

Client Name(s): _____

Address: _____

City: _____ State: _____ Zip: _____

Phone: Home: _____ Work: _____

           Cell: _____ Fax: _____

           E-mail: _____ Other: _____

Referral Fee: _____

Moving Date: _____

Appointment Date: _____

Comments:

_____
_____
_____
_____

_____   _____
Referring Agent   Date   Accepted By   Date

Delegation of Personal Chores

Remember the earliest mention in this book about the commitment to work five days and take two days off? Those two days are *not* for working at home or doing odd jobs around your office.

Delegation At Home

Delegation of personal chores is also critical in order to stay energized and moving forward. If you're going to be ready to hit it hard again on Monday morning, you need some time for:

- Relaxing
- Recreation
- Re-Charging

You do not clean your own house or your own office any more. You can delegate these tasks to somebody whose fee is much less that yours at the level we're moving you toward. You are no longer to:

- Mow your own lawn
- Wash your own windows
- Paint your own house
- Shampoo your own carpeting
- Stain your own deck
- Anything of this nature

I still do my own laundry and ironing, but I have these down to a fine science that's been a part of our Thursday night ritual for so long it feels okay. Our boys are grown and gone, so all we're talking about here is the *washable* stuff for two adults. Most of it goes to the dry cleaners, so it's just not that big a deal. While I'm working on these things, my husband generally pays bills or works on correspondence, and we may have a TV movie going, so it still *feels* like an evening of personal time.

I also still take my own car to the car wash, drop off and pick up dry cleaning, and stop at the grocery store, although I have noticed the way it's evolved over these last years that all three of these are at the same shopping plaza, which is located between our house and my office.

I know a lot of people who have their assistant handle all of these tasks, but they're at a much higher level of production, with more than one assistant. I'm not saying it's wrong to delegate all of this, I'm just saying that at the under $250,000 level, it doesn't seem to be much of an issue. What I am suggesting here is to delegate as much as you can that will help you stay on your Model Day schedule, and streamline your own efficiency at everything else.

Our house is always clean and orderly, our laundry never piles up, and I still have time to read two to three hours every evening, so I *know* it can be done. Do not be tempted to fall into the *"I can't afford it"* trap. Yes you can. If you're earning $150,000 or more annually, you can't afford *not* to spend $75 every two weeks to have somebody else come in and clean your house. The alternative is missing out on the fun you could be having with your family and friends by continuing to do it on your own on your day off, and you'll soon grow to resent that.

We still go around on Saturday doing errands for a couple of hours: grocery shopping, picking up dog food and pet supplies, etc. but we do this as sort of a ritual, too. This gives us some time together to talk and we go out for lunch, and maybe throw in a walk through downtown Flagstaff, which is historic and quaint and very charming. This is only a two to three hour deal, and with the fun thrown in, neither of us feels like we spent a day off doing just chores.

Part of the evolution of moving from a fairly ordinary income level to a much higher one obviously, is the shift to much higher productivity. But a lot of it is simply getting very good at blending things together so you're keeping all the balls in the air at the same time without ever feeling overwhelmed. A huge part of this is making that shift to taking two days off *no matter what* and then integrating fun and the little things that have to be done, so you *feel* like you're having a day off.

HAVE SYSTEMS AT HOME, TOO

This, too, relates to the importance of having systems in place. The whole idea is to have a way to do *everything* that's the same every time, so when it comes time to do it again, you don't have to make a big deal out of figuring out what to do and how to do it. One really *little* thing is just shopping at the same stores all the time, so you know your way around and can get in and out quickly and effortlessly.

That probably sounds corny, but think about it. Remember when you first had your own home and were just starting your adult life? Remember how important it seemed to get out all the grocery store ads and go around to every store and buy their best specials? It probably was important at the time, but now it's not even a consideration because you just can't invest that kind of time in something so basic.

If you know your regular grocery store, you can get in and out, even shopping for a full week, in probably thirty minutes. On the other hand, if you go all over town and have to hunt through each of five or six stores, you'll shoot a full half-day. If that use of time were going to save several hundred dollars, I guess I'd take a look at it, but for twenty bucks, it just doesn't make sense. If you have a teenager or college student in your family, you may want to take the time to teach them to shop, and just delegate the whole thing completely.

What else can be delegated? Again, incorporating the time and abilities of all members of your household, you may have resources for getting your car washed, ironing, getting younger children taken around and transported to various activities. Most teens will do just about anything for a chance to drive, so they will probably be very willing to help.

Again, the best rule of thumb is: any time a particular task begins to feel like a *recurring annoyance*, think about who else could do it. Then work your way through visualizing how you'd have them do it, and what's a fair price or a fair trade.

One of the things I appreciate most that I have completely delegated to someone else, is everything related to my real estate signs. I have a sign contractor who puts up and removes all my signs, all the time. I love it that he even stores them so I literally *never* think about them. I don't even know where they actually are, and don't have any reason to care.

Everybody I know who *doesn't* contract this service has the huge pain in the neck of a lot of signs creating a storage problem at their house or their office, or both, and they're constantly having to replace signs because they're always getting 'lost.' That's the polite term meaning they forgot to pick them up, which *always* irritates the new owner who, after he's sick of waiting for someone to pick it up, stashes it out behind his garage and it's never seen again.

Contracting for sign installation and maintenance is accounted for in your systems in place, and you just never have to give it much thought. Your assistant calls and orders a sign 'up' for each new listing, and 'down' for each sold and closed property, and maybe orders special riders in between for Pending, Sold But We Have Others, etc. There's nothing to it, and it's very inexpensive. My sign contractor charges about $15 for everything from start to finish for each listing. He provides, in my opinion, one of the most valuable services in our industry.

Hiring A Sign Contractor

If you don't have anybody who does this in your area, find somebody and offer to help them get started. The ideal candidate is somebody who has recently retired and doesn't particularly like not having something to do. You could help spread the word through your MLS and among your personal real estate friends and he could practically be in business overnight. All he really needs is:

- A post hole digger
- Some strips of rebar
- Screw drivers and a bag of screws
- A pick up truck
- A little garage and yard space
- That's it.

Chapter Fourteen:
Time-Sensitive Responsibilities

Top Priority

Now, what about those days off? Is there any work-related activity you might be willing to perform on a day off? As I've said repeatedly, my time off is pretty ruthlessly guarded, but there is *one* thing that must be taken pretty seriously at *all times,* and that is contract presentation.

To begin with, contracts are time-sensitive insofar as carrying an actual date and time by which a response must be made, or it will become void. Home fax machines having become quite common in recent years have been a big help, but we should be willing to accept responsibility for picking up the contract when faxing isn't possible, and at least reviewing it over the phone with our client. Usually that will suffice, with an in-person appointment scheduled for the next day before a response is formulated.

In my opinion, the clients deserve as much time as the contract deadline will allow to consider their response. Typically, this can be done without sending your family the message that they're no longer your priority of the day now that there's money to be made.

I've negotiated a ton of contracts over the years from my husband's parents' farm in the upper midwest, from my Mom's kitchen table, from various hotel rooms around the country while on vacation, and my family has been great about understanding the time-sensitivity of this activity.

Deliver Your Greatest Strength

Although I customarily have another agent cover most activity for me when I'm away, I *always* negotiate my own clients' contracts personally. I travel with a stack of fax cover sheets and Counter Offer forms. The greatest strength I bring to my clients, and the biggest reason they should list with me is that I am a *world-class negotiator*. Knowing that's where my nearly twenty-five years of experience can make a difference on their behalf, I feel I need to be there for them when the contract comes in, regardless of what I'm doing.

I once had three contracts on the same great house while attending my niece's wedding several states away. I did spend some time on the phone, but not during any of the actual wedding festivities, and not to the distraction of anyone else present. Now that everyone has cell phones, you can be called and notified about an in-coming contract without disrupting the whole environment. I'm sure my sister and her family were amazed at the number of calls I got that weekend, but I did try hard not to be disruptive, and they were all incredibly gracious. That was even before cell phones were as streamlined as they are now, and it still all worked out just fine.

A word about cell phones: they should *never* ring when we're with clients or at an event. You know how obnoxious someone looks when their cell phone rings at a seminar? We look just as obnoxious, even with an audience of one. Turn off the ringer and don't think about it again. You will *not* lose business, your company will not go under, and you'll be better off for having done so.

Just How Many Exceptions Are There?

What else would you be willing to do on a day off? What if you got a call at home telling you that somebody was standing on the door step of your listing, trying to show it, and their lock box key won't work? What about that? Are we going to start making exceptions for *everything*? No, just the *big* things that relate to our responsibility to do the job we promised to do. Getting the potential Buyer in that house at that moment is big, so yes; we have to go let them in.

You're surprised I said that, right? I just hope you're not confused. I don't want to do that. I want my message to be clear. It's either a work day or it isn't, but it's not a perfect world, and we do have to use some common sense. In the *"Lock box key doesn't work"* scenario, I'd ask who all of my family wants to ride along with me to solve that little dilemma. Chances are somebody might want to join me, and those who don't might take a second look at the invitation when they know we may stop for an iced cappuccino. See what I mean?

Six Figure Income

Use Common Sense

The whole idea is, don't spend all of your days off glued to the phone or your laptop, but be responsible. I frequently go for weeks without anything like that coming up, although contracts do come in on a regular basis. That's the number one thing on my Drop-everything-and-respond-list, but the fax machine and one call to the Seller are a very easy, manageable way to be responsible.

The goal, obviously, is to make sure you don't send your loved ones the message that you don't really mean what you say about prioritizing special time with them, while still maintaining high volume production. There are people who would argue that if you do *anything* work-related on a day off, then it's not a day off. For them, that's fine, but this works for me in my market place, with my systems and my philosophy and it still keeps me among the top producers in town. I think something similar will serve you well too.

The subject of this book, remember, is a system for people who want to make a nice comfortable six-figure income , without a huge entourage of help, without running themselves ragged every weekend and evening, and without surrendering their personal life. Any of the levels we've discussed can be managed nicely with one great assistant, a reliable colleague to refer business to, and some electronic conveniences. Honestly, it really does come down to just that one simple principle. I promise you, if you set your boundaries, and know your responsibilities, you can master this easier than you think.

Chapter Fifteen:
Experience = Better Profitability

Don't Be A Rookie Very Long

The best advice I can give you, is pay attention to all learning opportunities *early* and don't be a rookie very long. For those of you who have been in the business awhile, don't be a novice to this system very long.

By following the overall philosophy of successfully completing your daily prospecting, and incorporating the other disciplined activities of a successful agent, you'll become experienced quickly. These include:

- Practicing your scripts and dialogs
- Internalizing them
- Becoming highly visible

By doing these you'll acquire a good amount of quality experience in a hurry, then you can do a couple of things that will make a *huge* difference in your business without changing your life very much.

The Fifty Pound Fish

Experience is the best confidence builder in the world, and that's what it takes to list and sell higher priced homes. To quote my favorite CRS instructor, Del Bain again, *"If you want to catch fifty pound fish, you have to go where the fifty pound fish are."* In our case, the fifty pound fish are the higher priced homes with higher commissions. If they're *your* listings, you can be sure you're always paid the commission *you* charge, even if everybody around you is reducing theirs.

Look at the comparison of figures we used earlier for the agent on the 60/40 split, and what you can do with the confidence you gain from experience. We said the average sale price in town was $175,000, but the new agent with no experience will very likely start with some $125,000 sales. This could also be true for a seventeen-year veteran who, in reality has one year of experience, seventeen times. Maybe that $125,000 home is listed at a 5% commission, averaged in with properties that are listed at 6%, so we used a 2.7% figure for the selling side. Their average earned commission was $3.375, but they only got 60%, so they were actually paid $2,025. If they averaged two sales per month, totaling twenty-four in a year, their annualized gross income was $48,600.

When you have more experience and can confidently list at 6% because you know your service is worth it and can expect to be working at the full value of the $175,000 average sale price, your earned commission on the listing side is 3% of $175,000, or $5,250. If you've had the confidence to negotiate successfully with your Broker, or to move to a 100% office, you actually get paid the full $5,250. By doing thirty transactions, only six more than your former rookie status, look what happens to your income: $5,250 x 30 = $157,500. Over *three times* the gross revenue, with only six more sales.

You'll lose half of it to taxes and expenses in either case, but I'd much rather have $78,500 left for my effort than $24,300, and your personal life is virtually unchanged. With a good assistant, you can actually double your volume from your first couple of rookie years, and here's what the math looks like: $5,250 x 48 = $252,000 total income. This can still be done in five days, without working nights. If you're tempted to run the math out much higher, of course it can be done. There are a lot of people who do much more than this, but as you know by now, my philosophy is to keep it simple, avoid over-complicating, and bigger numbers do necessitate a lot more of everything.

Keeping It Simple

The higher the numbers, the more help you need, then the more equipment you need, the bigger and therefore more expensive ads you need, and more expensive office space you need, and the next thing you know, you've got new management challenges. You've got more complications because you've built a brokerage business *within* a brokerage business. If that's what you want, more power to you, but that's not for me. I'm with Del Bain, *"I want more in my pocket and less on my mind."* For me, less really is more.

Obviously, the best way to increase your income without complicating your life is to raise your average sale price and still do the same number of units. Also, get good at listing, so you'll be in charge of your commission rate. As you know, commissions are strictly negotiable and cannot be set by any body or group of professionals, but there are just too many people out there who are not treating their business like a business, and are caving in to the pressure for

Six Figure Income

reduced commissions.

If you sell their listings, you'll make less money. I would never let the commission affect a showing decision, however. I think the Buyer deserves to see the homes that meet their needs without regard to the commission, but I prefer the backbone of my business to be from listings, and this is one of the reasons. The other, obviously, is that time management is much easier to deal with if you're a heavy lister.

So back to raising your average sale price: 3% of $200,000 = $6,000 x 30 closings = $180,000, or at 40 closings = $240,000. That's not that hard to do, and the work effort is *one hundred percent identical.* Remember the statistics you've been gathering on a regular basis from your MLS staff? This is what all that information is for: *now* you can go where the fifty pound fish are.

Chances are, many of the readers of this book are people who have been in the business awhile, but are either not making the money they know they'd like to make, or are working all the time and don't have any kind of personal life. If you're one of them, maybe your farming effort has been sporadic, and needs to be fine-tuned. If you're experienced, you know *exactly* where the fifty pound fish are.

Turning Up The Heat

Choose a few neighborhoods with the sale price you want to work in, and get your newsletter going. I really want to encourage you to strongly consider fifteen hundred households. Yes, it is expensive, and yes, it takes some time to build, but you'll get *some* response right away the first year, possibly enough to pay for the investment and return a profit *if you are consistent and work a big enough area.* Promise yourself that once you start, you will not allow any excuse not to continue.

We know that a fifteen hundred-piece mailing done monthly is about a $10,000 annual investment, but remember, you don't have to pay that all at once. Look at it this way, this is the single strongest business generator that will increase your numbers enough to allow you to negotiate for 100% commissions. In doing so, your average commission will go from $2,025 to $5,250 using the numbers in our example. Two sales will pay for your newsletter and put you on your way to dramatically increasing your income, and here's the key: *without disrupting your personal life.*

100% Commissions

For any Brokers who are mad at me for putting such ideas in the heads of your sales force, I would ask you to consider what is really in the best interest of a serious long-term career agent. How about this, rather than lose your best people, why not give them the option of being 100% agents? Charge them their fair share of the office expenses, say $1,200 per month and let them pay all of their own expenses. Let them know exactly what they're buying:

- Their office space
- Errors and omissions insurance
- Full-Time receptionist and support staff
- Phone and voice mail system
- Use of a lot of expensive office equipment
- Avoidance of their own franchise fee
- The ability to earn 100% commissions

I don't care what anybody says, your agent *cannot* set up and maintain a high-class professional office for $14,000 on their own. Period. In anybody's language, that is a very fair deal.

From your standpoint, if you have ten agents on this program, $140,000 should contribute very nicely to your overhead, and twenty at $280,000 should turn a profit for you. Think about it. It could be an *everybody wins* situation.

Take Your Commitment Seriously

Agents, I'll repeat again, unless you really like management and are prepared to get out of sales and do it right, *don't* become the Broker. They are two completely different jobs, two completely different lives, and if you can negotiate something like this, do it. You'll both be better off in the long run.

You do need to understand that once you go on the 100% program, you're there permanently. You can't ask to flip-flop back and forth if your business fluctuates and expect your Broker to be able to run a financially sound operation that you can expect will always be there for you. So don't take this lightly, and don't ask to do this prematurely. When you do make the commitment, put in an honest work effort, follow your business plan and marketing campaign like a religion, and you'll be just fine.

Maintaining Good Office Relations

How do you keep your office colleagues from freaking out when you take this option and pull way out ahead of them? In some cases you may not, but the really good agents don't care what anybody else is doing, and the main thing is just don't talk about it much, and *never* rub it in.

Gently educate a few of your office friends that you're building your business mostly around listings. Tell them you're taking a few selected Buyers, and that you're referring out most of your sign and ad calls. You'll want your 25% referral fee, which is much different than just letting the floor person take them.

Here's what you're offering: 40 to 50 listings a year at $200,000 listed at 6% on each side. That will generate $60,000 to $75,000 potentially to you in referral fees, if you can keep most of those prospects in house and $180,000 to $225,000 to the other agents who sell them. Why not gear your marketing so most of them can be your office colleagues? Obviously, you've done very well on the listing side: 40 listings = $240,000 and 50 listings = $300,000.

On the selling side, agents from other offices will sell some of those listings. But if say, just twenty of them end up in house on your referral system and you take 25%, you'll add $1,500 x 20 = $30,000 to your annual income, which will make a nice contribution to your expenses. Best of all, nothing changes. You have no time investment, you don't need any more office space, no more help, nor more equipment, nada. What a concept!

If you can keep a lot of those prospects in house, you could refer out enough business to keep two or three of your office colleagues very happy. Please trust me on this and do it this way. Please don't be tempted to hire a bunch of Buyer Agents to work for you. You will complicate your life unnecessarily, and your expenses will go way up.

Chapter Sixteen:
Re-Evaluation: Is This What You Really Want?

A Second Look

Now that we've seen the overall plan and are aware of the work effort required, logistics, and the commitment of time and expense necessary to building a successful business, let's look again at what we *thought* we wanted.

> **GOALS RE-EVALUATION**
>
> Review your goals, and ask yourself again:
>
> - Why do I want to earn a six-figure income?
> - Why is this important ?
> - What will it do for me?
> - What is meaningful to me?
>
> Let's measure those answers against:
>
> - Am I clear on the price I will have to pay?
> - Does my work ethic match my dream?
> - Am I as committed as the work requires?
> - Am I okay with the changes that will result?

We also need to look at how we'll structure our business to achieve our goals and dreams. *It is absolutely vital here to get our egos out of the way.* It's easy to get caught up in the excitement of running the math out to exponential heights and create a *huge* business, and that's fine, but we need some reality checks. Certainly, this is not done to limit the scope of our thinking; our only purpose for re-evaluation is to be sure this is absolutely what we want.

COMPARE THE NUMBERS

As I've expressed often, I am a proponent of keeping it as simple as possible and avoiding the temptation to over-complicate. This philosophy is the experienced result of my own mistakes. You may need to make some of your own before you know what's right for you, but I'd sure like to help you minimize them.

Six Figure Income

Everything Has A Price

Here's a comparison that may help:

    50 Transactions x $5,250 = $262,500

    One assistant earning*   38,704

    20% other expenses   52,500

    Net taxable income: $171,296

    100 Transactions x $5,250 = $525,000

    4 assistants @ $50K ea.**   200,000

    28% other expenses   147,000

    Net taxable income: $178,000

*Calculation of Unlicensed Assistant's Compensation:

    $12 per hour x 40 hours x 52 weeks = $24,960

    x 115% to include withholdings = $28,704

    + $200 per closing x 50 = $10,000

    Total paid to assistant = $34,960

    Your cost including withholdings = $38,704

**4 Assistants= 1 office administrator, 3 licensed people averaging $50,000 each.

Has there ever been a time in your life that you've worried about how you were going to make your house payment or your car payment? I think most of us know that feeling and have been there at some time or other.

That's something you need to consider every time you are thinking about adding a new staff member. Each time you hire another person, you take on the responsibility of *their* house payment and *their* car payment. People come to depend on their jobs to pay their bills, and we need to understand, they're not coming to work to build *our* career, from their perspective, they work to earn their own livelihood.

True, we can't do it all without help, and you may very well choose to build a fairly sizeable business. There are some legendary producers out there who are doing phenomenal things. This is your business and you need to do it your way; these are simply thoughts I'd like you to be aware of as you make your decision.

Staff compensation and the directly proportionate need for more equipment and more office space, along with the additional complications and management challenges are the reason I am such a strong proponent of outsourcing and sticking to one assistant.

Reviewing The Components Of Production

Having revisited these important questions, you've now decided to move forward in *your* way toward the realization of your personal goals and dreams. Looking at ways to build your business will include a combination of your marketing plan and strict disciplined daily attention to your business plan.

Above all else, stay focused on your prospecting. This is something that *must* be done faithfully every day. Without it, very little else will happen. Any time you hit a stretch where your closings are down, if you look back sixty to ninety days, you'll see that there wasn't enough prospecting going on. Conversely, if you do a lot of prospecting and you're faithful and consistent with it, you'll see very strong closing activity in the *next* sixty to ninety days.

Remember that your prospecting needs to be done early in the day. A lot of people will tell you that nobody's home in the mornings, and if you're worried about that, go to their place of business. We talked about door-knocking, but doing it from your ABC list, instead of going door-to-door in a residential area. That works. If you talk to a lot of people every day about what you sell, you'll sell a lot of it.

You need to be very tough on pricing. Stay on top of what's going on in your market, and check weekly to make sure every listing you have is still priced right. If not, talk to your Sellers early and often about price reductions and changes in market conditions. Price is the *only* issue in real estate. It will account for any discrepancy with any property any time, whether it's:

- Age
- Location
- Condition

Some people won't want to paint or replace carpeting when you advise them to do so, which will lose a significant number of prospects because they've eliminated the chance to make a great first impression. For those people, price reductions are critical, and only the market can tell you if they need more than one.

Stay on top of this faithfully and take the initiative to contact your Sellers *first* before they call you. If they have to call you, their perception is going to be that you're not doing your job, and I guarantee you, they'll interpret that to mean you're not interested in them *or* their house. Do not let this happen, or they'll cancel, list with somebody else, give them the price reduction *you* asked for, and it'll sell.

Tracking By The Numbers

You're keeping track of your numbers all the time now, so you know your ratios of *everything:*

- Calls to leads
- Leads to appointments
- Appointments to listings
- Listings to closings

Study them and pay close attention to what they tell you. For example, if you really are doing a lot of prospecting, but are not getting very many good leads, you may not be making enough *high impact* calls. In other words, calls to people with a known real estate need: FSBOs and Expireds.

If you're not getting enough appointments, that may be a signal that you need more script practice. If you're not getting enough listings, you probably need to practice your listing presentation. You may want to consider the exercise in brutal honesty of video taping your listing presentation.

There are all kinds of signals that can really help you improve if you look at it that way. Maintain very high standards in all of these areas and be completely honest with yourself, and stay focused on the rewards.

> **REVIEW YOUR BUSINESS PLAN WEEKLY**
>
> That's why I believe it's so important to have:
>
> - Written goals
> - Visual reminders
> - Written affirmations
> - Affirmations recorded in your own voice
> - A written business plan

Scheduling is another critical element of building to high-volume production. In my opinion, there is great value in scheduling the most critical tasks of the day to be completed before noon. That does two valuable things:

- It assures that they'll get done
- Scheduling revenue generators is easier

There are just too many things that can and will come up, and they all seem important. That will prevent completion of the things we discussed when we talked about the Model Day. With the Revenue Instigators (prospecting in all forms) scheduled in the morning, you automatically know you have all afternoon for the 'Revenue Generators' (listing appointments and the occasional Preferred Buyer appointment).

You just know automatically that you're booked solid in the morning, but you have all afternoon, starting at 12:00 Noon and continuing through 6:00 or 7:00 for appointments with clients. If you can fill all or even most of those time slots, you will have all the business you could possibly manage.

STAY FOCUSED ON MINDSET

Mindset is probably 95% of the battle here. Read good motivational books with accounts of people who have done great things, and you'll see time and again, the common thread of perseverance and commitment. If you really want to build a great business, get in the habit of being around people who are doing more than you are, and observe carefully. Learn all you can about their:

- Work Ethic

Six Figure Income

- Behaviors
- Habits
- Attitudes

In addition to reading, I really feel you should be listening to tapes constantly to help you with the mindset of success, and to help you realize that it's all possible and that you're as worthy and deserving as *anyone*.

The *simple version* of the way to take a jump in production is:

- Decide what you want
- Determine the steps to get there
- Set a realistic time-frame

In deciding what you want, make it very specific, very detailed, be realistic, don't be limited by anyone else's beliefs. In determining the steps to get there, again, the more specific and detailed, the better. Here, you will pay very careful attention to having systems in place for everything, and to what things you can out-source or delegate.

Next, set a realistic time-frame. I learned a long time ago from Mike Ferry that we all tend to *overestimate* what we can do short term, but *underestimate* what we can do long term. Isn't that a great thought. Experience over several years has confirmed that there is tremendous wisdom in that statement.

Give this careful consideration, paying attention to each individual component and you'll know where to set your goals. Gradual continued experience will show you how to increase them for sustainable growth over an extended period of years.

Finally, have the courage to measure your progress by critiquing yourself *honestly* with the determination and the expectation of continuing to improve. Don't get discouraged. Any time you feel like you may be getting discouraged, start calling your past clients. They'll tell you how pleased they are with their homes, with *you,* with your follow-up, and with the continuation of the courtesy and kindness you extend to them.

Chapter Seventeen:
Revolutionizing Retail Sales

The Jewelry Broker

This chapter will discuss applying the principles of real estate sales to retail selling. I believe that doing so would allow those engaged in retail sales to move their endeavor from a *job* to a *career* and bring them enormous satisfaction.

I have fantasized more than once over the years, that if the real estate industry ever changed so dramatically that I felt I couldn't or didn't want to be a part of it, I would fashion myself a new career as a Jewelry Broker for somebody else's store.

I would assemble a list of everybody I ever heard of, mostly business and professional men, who probably have the means, but maybe neither the time nor the know-how to shop artfully for the ladies in their lives.

Gifts For All Reasons

My goal would be to have two hundred-fifty clients, each making four purchases a year for gifts for:

- Christmas or Hanukkah
- Birthday
- Valentine's Day
- Their Anniversary

> **ESPECIALLY FOR HER**
>
> I would interview each client and take massively detailed notes regarding many pieces of information about the lady in their lives, such as:
>
> - The colors she most often wears
> - Places they like to go
> - Events they attend
> - Description of the watch, rings, and other jewelry worn daily

KING OF DREAMS

I would ask for photos of her, and I would train my clients to listen for subtle hints or clues that could become gift suggestions. I would keep incredibly detailed electronic files, with a back-up copy in my safe deposit box at the bank, with all of this glorious and useful information. All of this is designed to make him the *King of her Dreams,* and all he has to do is sign the card.

We would meet face-to-face twice a year, at his work place, and confer by phone for the other two gifts. In all cases, they would be delivered magnificently gift wrapped, to his work place, complete with a beautiful carefully selected card, ready for his personal message.

Men who do not really enjoy shopping, and those who are unsure of themselves regarding selection of gifts, will value this service enormously. The owner of the jewelry store will hire you on the spot, on a commission basis, because of the huge boost in sales volume you will be creating.

Although Flagstaff is small, we do have quite a nice mall with a great Dillard's Department Store, as well as unusually good JC Penny's and Sears stores. I would be so pleased and proud if some of their sales associates would use these ideas to take a similar approach in increasing their personal sales volume.

I believe it would be well-received if someone went to their store manager and asked the store to pay for personal business cards and a nice high-quality note card with which they could offer to help with the selection of gifts for these four major occasions. This note card would be sent to the entire Chamber of Commerce membership, and all professionals, concentrating mostly on men, because so many of them want and appreciate help with this sort of thing.

Management should really require that the associate follow each piece of mail with a phone call to schedule a specific appointment to make the gift selections. During the phone interview, the client would be asked his wife's or girlfriend's:

- Sizes

- Color preferences

- Favorite designers and brands

The initial mailing would tell them to expect the forthcoming call, and to please look in her closet ahead of time, check the labels, note the colors, and be prepared with this information. The client would then set an appointment to come in and make their selections.

Dillard's has a Santa Hint Card that works very well, but the *recipient* actually makes the gift selection, which takes at least *some* of the element of surprise out of it, which in my opinion, is a huge part of the fun of both giving and receiving a gift.

The store should be prepared to help coordinate some semblance of order to the scheduling of appointments to make sure these *personally invited* customers are made to feel incredibly special. Plenty of gift wrapping help should be in place, and a delivery option offered. I'm not suggesting that the store *give* anything away. I'm watching the bottom line and recommending extra services for which I believe the preferred customer will gladly pay.

The delivery option may or may not be a huge deal. In a small town where the commute time is not an issue, most customers would be very willing to come back later to pick up their beautifully wrapped gifts. These same courtesies could obviously be extended to women who shop in the men's department.

The sales associate would keep files with all of this information, and should be required to send a Thank You note (after the holiday, so no surprise would ever be spoiled). If I were the manager, I would have the sales associate write the notes, but I would do the mailing myself, to make sure they were actually sent, thus inviting the repeat business.

Of course, the store would have the master files so that in the event of a sales associate's departure, another associate could follow through, retaining the business for the store. This would also ensure the continuation of helping the customer who values the service.

This approach to retail selling truly does create an *everybody wins* situation. The store's increased sales volume is obviously great for business, and the extended customer service is tremendously valuable for the customers themselves, which promotes customer loyalty. From the perspective of the sales associate, this elevates their position from simply clerking, to a *creative sales career,* bringing with it a personal satisfaction which will greatly enhance the way they feel about what they do. Again, that benefits the store as well, because people stay in career positions longer and find them more satisfying.

Become A 'Hero Maker'

The Flagstaff Mall also has a great Sears store with a hardware and tools department guaranteed to make men salivate just walking though it. We can only guess what would happen if a sharp sales associate or two created a similar program geared toward assisting women with the selection of gifts for the men in their lives. My husband would practically *worship* a well-trained salesperson who could help him get the tools and outdoor gear that make his heart sing.

Even I, who love shopping so much that I have gone on record as proclaiming that I want to be buried at Scottsdale Fashion Square, would participate in such a program in order to please my husband with gifts he would love.

If I worked in the Sears tools and sporting goods departments, I would take this a step farther. I would offer to come to your house, inventory your husband's tools, and get you on a program to fill in anything he doesn't already have, based on the hobbies, etc. you tell me the tools would be used for.

We also have an exceptional JC Penny's store, which in my humble but correct opinion, does a spectacular job with their offering of winter coats and jackets. These items, too, lend themselves very well to gift-giving, especially at Christmas and Hanukkah. Here again, if I were a sales associate there, I would go outside the store to bring in business. I would make sure it came directly to me by invitation, and by appointment, obviously with management approval and support.

If you are that associate, even if you aren't paid on commission, I'm sure you are either paid or recognized in some other way for your personal sales volume. Talk to your store manager and get the store excited about letting you create your *Preferred Customer Program*, and increasing the store's overall sales volume.

Now that I've already blurted out in front of what I *hope* is the entire world (the readership of this book.) that I'm wild about Scottsdale Fashion Square, let me say that I do an awful lot of shopping at the Flagstaff Mall. For two years running, I was able to do all of my Christmas shopping, except a Cabela's catalog order, here in town. That's important for small towns especially, and I hope this section of this book will help others keep some of the business at home, so to speak.

Nothing would please me more than to have had a hand in providing the inspiration for some energetic sales associates who have a desire to serve, both their employers and their customers, to take these ideas and run with them. There's huge potential for:

➣ Satisfaction

➣ Recognition

➣ Personal Rewards

Changing your job to a satisfying career by doing this, holds potential for the betterment of everyone concerned. The next pages are a blue print for putting your plan together.

Jewelry Broker's Action Plan

Goal: 250 satisfied clients, each making 4 major gift purchases annually:

- Chamber of Commerce membership directory
- List of all the attorneys in town
- List of all the physicians in town
- List of all the dentists in town
- List of all the accountants in town
- List of all the real estate brokers in town
- List of all the business owners in town
- List of all the teachers in town
- List of all the university professors in town
- List of all the managers in town
- List of all the bankers in town
- List of all the car dealers in town
- List of all the contractors in town
- List of all the retired people in town
- List of all the association members in town
- List of all the media people in town
- List of all the insurance people in town
- List of all the service business people in town
- Lists of everyone else I may have overlooked

These categories are designed to jog your memory and to help point out that your best client could be *anywhere*. With a goal of 250 happy, satisfied clients, you may need an initial list of 1,000 or more for your prospecting.

Initial contact: If you can afford it, a nice invitation, similar to a graduation announcement or wedding invitation, would be nice. Otherwise, use a professionally printed flyer to introduce your idea.

INITIAL CONTACT

Something like this:

> "Jane Smith is pleased to announce that she is now affiliated with Big Gems Jewelers as a professional jewelry broker. Her mission is to make you *The King of Your Lady's Dreams* on all your future gift giving occasions. Jane will call you in the next few days regarding your participation in this confidential program."

SENDING MANAGEABLE QUANTITIES:

The rule for this type of mailing is in the key words *"calling you within the **next few days**."* Every piece of this mailing that is sent out *must* be followed with a phone call within three to four days at most.

Commit to sending twenty per week, mailing them on Saturday, so you can begin your follow-up calls on Monday. Try to be done by Wednesday, so you have Thursday and Friday to take care of any call backs that may arise.

These are all hand addressed, in your very best penmanship, and we are using commemorative stamps. Go to the Post Office and pick out the most creative and artistic stamps they have to offer.

Six Figure Income

Phone Script for the Follow-Up Calls:

Phone Script

This is Jane Smith, jewelry broker, with Big Gem Jewelers. Did you receive the announcement about our King of Dreams program? _____ We're very excited about helping busy professional men with selection, wrapping, and delivery of gifts for the special lady in your life. Our service is designed to help you with gifts for Christmas or Hanukkah, her birthday, Valentine's Day, and your anniversary, and *we do it all for you,* with no work on your part, and it's all *completely confidential,* of course. May I ask you a few questions regarding the gifts you like to give her? _____ What types of things have you done in the past?

When is her Birthday? _____   When is your Anniversary? _____

Does she prefer Silver or Gold? _____ Favorite Gem? _____

I'd like to bring a few samples over to show you, would you prefer a morning or afternoon appointment? _____

Using this script, in this order, you have *briefly* described your program, and you have avoided asking *"are you interested?"* because without knowing more, he may say, *"No, thank you."* By asking *"When is her Birthday?"* you can gauge by his answer whether or not he may be interested. Referring to *busy professional men* suggests the idea that this is for people who do not have much time for shopping.

When asking for the appointment, don't ask, *"May I come by to show you some samples?"* because that, too, allows the option of *"No, thank you."* This is why you simply *state* that you would like to come by, and you're asking for a preference of morning or afternoon.

If you get any resistance, that would be the time to say that you wouldn't anticipate that it would take more than twenty or thirty minutes. Start with people you know, so you'll be more likely to be granted the appointment, and learn from these initial calls and appointments how you may want to adjust, if necessary.

The script is actually written out on a card, and is used each and every time you make a call. Use pre-printed cards to record the information and take the card with you on the appointment to add to it.

The Appointment

➤ Introduce yourself, and hand him your card

➤ Show the samples

➤ Explain the program exactly as it is outlined at the beginning of this chapter. Sell the benefits of saving time and expertise in gift selection, *based on his input.*

Tell your new client that you will check in with him four weeks before any of the gift-giving occasions, to discuss ideas, price range, and particulars. Then tell him you will make the selection, bring it over for his approval two weeks ahead, and return with the wrapped gift and a card for his signature five days before the occasion.

Department Store Associate's Action Plan

Your prospect list begins with the same list of lists to help you determine who you know well, and who you feel you would like to have as preferred clients. Prospecting is done in a two-step process, first the mailing, then the follow-up call, and in your case, because you have much more to sell than strictly jewelry, you may want to add a third step.

Remember that in your phone call you are telling your prospect that before he comes into the store he should look in his wife or girlfriend's closet for:

➤ Sizes

➤ Color preferences

➤ Favorite brands and designers

Your third step would be to offer, in the phone conversation, to send him a post card to record this information. Put a stamp on it and ask him to drop it in the mail at least three days before his appointment, so you can have some items pre-selected for his choices and final approval.

This will give you two gauges to determine how strong your prospect actually is. The first will be his response to your offer to send the post card. If he says he would be interested in having you do that, he's probably a pretty good prospect. The second would be determined by his actually sending it in. If he does that, you know you have a very solid prospect. The post card, incidentally, would be sent inside a note or flyer, thanking him for his interest in the program, and stressing that your objectives are to help him save time and make him a hero with his gifts.

Your number of clients goal may be significantly different from that of the jewelry broker, who has no other store-related duties, while you have many. You can probably get your best guidance from your store manager in this regard. This will tell you how big your list of prospects needs to be and how many announcements you need to send out.

General Tips

- Get the price break point for your announcements from the printer
- This will be 200, 250, or 300
- To keep the cost down, order the smallest of those quantities
- Make arrangements to re-order as needed
- Prioritize your list beginning with the people you know best first
- Send to your most likely prospects first
- Progress through your list, always focusing on most likely
- As in any other sales career, make your prospecting calls early
- Do a very thorough job of follow-up
- Keep excellent, detailed records on each client

Good luck with this great venture. I wish you much success and satisfaction.

Chapter Eighteen:
How Life Balance Reflects the Why

Re-Focus on Mindset

As we discussed at the beginning of this book, aside from work ethic, the mindset of financial success is without question the single most crucial key to achieving it. Reading books by the great authors who have made it their life's study will help you stay focused on *how* to achieve success, as well as keeping in the front of your mind *why* you do what it takes.

Listen to tapes all the time. Learn everything you can about affirmations. Make a cassette tape of your affirmations in your own voice, and listen to it every morning on your way to work.

If you are ever feeling *off* and need to re-focus, stop and read your affirmations out loud. Then write them out on a beautiful piece of stationery to keep in front of you as you continue on throughout your day. Remember that your affirmations can be adjusted as needed along the way. Remember also that they are positive statements made from the perspective of having already accomplished your goals, and that your subconscious accepts as truth anything you tell it, which is why these are such a powerful tool.

Also, stay focused on the *why* by reviewing your goals often and paying particular attention to the Why section of your business plan. Take some time each day to pay attention to the details of your Treasure Map. These are all things that, once internalized into your belief system, will begin to feel natural to you, and your daily habits will begin to lead you toward the *expectation* of achieving them.

This is very important to the achievement of *any* success, but particularly so if you are the first person in your family or social group to achieve at a high level. I think most people realize that it's quite likely that they'll earn more money than the previous generation, but what about living a completely different lifestyle from everyone else in your family? Are you okay with that? Again, reviewing this section of your business plan where you asked yourself those important questions will help you.

First, you'll probably never actually come right out and mention specific figures, just like you wouldn't name drop. You'll still love the same people, you'll still want to share the same great experiences, and do the same fun things, but now you'll be able to do *more things* and give *more gifts* than you could before.

Be generous, but don't ruin everybody else's ability to enjoy being with you by always insisting on picking up the tab. Remember to give others the chance to reciprocate by realizing that everybody enjoys the same satisfaction in doing so. If there's something incredibly special you want to do for someone, do it at a time that you can most easily get away with it, without having it seem out of place, such as their birthday.

If you're worried about this, the most comforting thing I can tell you is that it won't happen overnight. You'll have a chance to grow into it gradually and get comfortable with it. While it is *possible* to go from modest, or even zero production to $100,000 or more in one year, it's far *more likely* to take two years, and you'll have plenty of business expenses in the earliest building years to keep you humble. Then there's the *tax hit,* so you, along with the people closest to you, will have a gradual adjustment to your newfound abundance. A word of caution: get with your accountant right out of the block and make a proper provision for that *tax hit*. Many real estate people neglect this, and create all sorts of problems for themselves. April 15th is *not* an emergency. It comes every year and we have to be prepared for it.

The Individuality of Spending Habits

You'll prioritize along the way what's important to you and where you'll feel okay spending money. This is *so individual,* and it's interesting to watch in ourselves and others. I'm sure there are people who are appalled at the money I spend on clothes and at the beauty shop for hair and nails, and I, of course, have opinions on some of the spending habits I see. We human beings are such interesting creatures.

As an example, you will *never* catch me with one of those $400-$500 designer purses everybody swears by. One of our sons had a girlfriend a few years ago who forgot one of those in a house she moved out of, and we never saw her again, so I still have it. I left the house with it a couple of times, and found myself offering lengthy explanations and half-apologies because I literally couldn't stand having anybody think I had no respect for the work effort required to earn the price of something so frivolous. An yet, if there were a twelve-step recovery program for people who buy too many dishes, I'd have to go. Spending habits are, indeed, very individual.

A few years ago, as a part of the annual ritual of getting ready to go to Mike Ferry's Superstar Retreat, we started the tradition of a weekend in Phoenix during which I would shop to my heart's content. The mission was three nice business outfits, complete with shoes, underwear, and full accessories, so it was a *splendid* experience. The timing of this was perfect, because it came close to the end of summer when everything was on sale, and those pur-

Six Figure Income

chases became the start of next summer's wardrobe. Nonetheless, this was by no means an *inexpensive* weekend.

The first time I really kicked into high gear, and filled the entire back end of the Suburban with packages, Brad, who didn't want to come right out and ask, *"My God. How much **did** you spend?"* commented good-naturedly about the apparent success of the mission. This was about the time then-President Bill Clinton had outraged a fair percentage of the population with the rumors about his $200 hair cuts, or so the tabloids said. On our way home, still refraining from asking for a figure, Brad asked if I'd found everything I was hoping for, and I replied, *"Yes, and it wasn't much more than the price of a few haircuts."*

What Makes Your Heart Sing?

What makes *your* heart sing? Would you love to be so successful that you could play a $250 round of golf regularly and never give it a second thought? Would you like a closet full of those purses I can't even deal with? Do you dream of four vacations a year, each to some incredibly exciting destination? Is a classic old car your secret dream? How about a second home in whatever you define as the most beautiful place on earth?

Initially, I suspect that most of us just want to get out of debt, comfortably be able to pay our bills, make a few investments, and put some money in the bank. What about after that? There truly are *no limits,* and you really can do *anything* you want to do.

Even if nobody in your family or your circle of friends has ever done anything like this before, it's okay for you to do it. As Mark Victor Hansen says, *"If everybody's going to be better off, and nobody's going to be worse off, there's no reason not to move forward and just go on ahead with it."* Don't you just love that philosophy? It's not going to harm anyone, not going to take anything away from anyone else, and it's going to make a lot of things better, so let's just go on ahead and succeed.

Put this someplace where you'll see it every day. Add it to your Treasure Map, or put it in your affirmations, or better yet, at the top of the call sheets you use every day for your prospecting. It seems incredibly simple, but it's actually quite profound, and it will help keep you focused on the mindset of success. It will help you internalize more deeply *why* you're willing to do the things you need to do, with the intention and the expectation of being successful.

Smelling the Roses... Really.

A very interesting thing happened to me just last summer: a *ten-plus* on the scale of life's big *"Aha"* moments. I met a group of incredible people at a writers' retreat in Sedona, Arizona, with Tom Bird...just twenty-eight miles from Flagstaff, so practically right in my own back yard. The participants came from all over the country and brought with them the warmest, most loving, and inspiring spirit of joy and sharing I have ever experienced in my entire life.

All this time, I've been patting myself on the back for being what I had genuinely believed was one of the few really life-balanced, strong producing real estate agents. I thought life balance meant *not working seven days a week*. Wow! How naive. Sharing that week with those folks was a real eye-opener.

I had the feeling, though nothing was ever said aloud, that I was the only person in attendance who had never experienced the world as a place of such utter beauty and deep contentment. Those people had been *everywhere* and tried every neat experience you could imagine. Nobody was judgmental, and nobody tried to inflict their values, beliefs, and experiences on anyone else. But as I interacted with them, I found myself thinking, *"Wow! Look at what I've been missing."* This from a true detail person who really *does* appreciate and enjoy a lot of things.

Please bear in mind that I had, until that time, been the Queen of Self-Satisfaction and had some *definite* opinions about many entrepreneurs who I believed were far less balanced than I because they would drop everything and go off on a chase anytime their pager went off. Not I. I threw my pager away eight years ago, and I've already told you how I schedule both *days on* and *days off a full year at a time.*

But what about the things that *could* be done evenings and those days off? I'm an insatiable reader - good for about a hundred books a year - so obviously, that's a daily activity, done in the evening. I do appreciate enormously that I'm a very high energy person, and don't need a lot of sleep. Still...what about *early* evening and those days off?

We're real big on short trips pretty often, and I'm a world-class shopper who truly finds as much joy in the experience as in the purchases. Doing these two things regularly had perpetuated the naive myth in my mind that this was life-balance. Oh yes, and we need to throw in that I'm a TV Snob and don't approve of just blindly staring into the TV irrespective of what's on. So, I thought it was good that I rarely waste time on this, also contributing to my smugly presumed Life Balance.

Imagine my shock at listening to my new friends at the writers' retreat, sharing insights on what's beautiful to them, what's fun, what's joyful. I had no idea so many little things could have meaning...significance...specialness. It was so inspiring to hear of their travels, their unbelievably varied and interesting hobbies, their simple and sometimes pretty elaborate interests.

I found myself one day recently, after thinking about all this, making a list of things I loved to do *before I became so completely absorbed in entrepeneurship*. Don't get me wrong: I have loved it, and it has been very good to me. In addition to my own rewards, it's allowed me to help a lot of people realize their own piece of the American Dream. I expect I'll continue for some time; it's just that now, I'm thinking a lot more about smelling the roses, which I thought I'd been doing all along.

I'm starting to think about going to the fabric shops to find the perfect Country French print for a long round table cloth for our dining room. Once I've made that, I've got a great idea for a centerpiece combining some gorgeous silk poppies I found in Santa Fe and an exquisite vase we received as a wedding gift from a special friend.

I'm excited about the fun I'll have arranging, in a new cabinet, collections of Teddy Bears and antique children's tea sets, among them, my Grandmother's, my Mom's, my own from childhood, along with a number of others lovingly collected over the years. The Teddy Bears will be wearing big hats and jewelry for their 'Teas,' which will allow for a wonderfully creative adventure, and frankly, an opportunity to *play*. What a joy. I've been absorbed by career success for so long that I'd lost sight of the therapeutic value of play.

True, we go to a lot of concerts, baseball games, and other event offerings here and in Phoenix, but when you're essentially hanging out *entirely* with other entrepreneurs, chances are that's what will determine the topic of conversation. It will also be the mindset and outlook that will accompany you everywhere you go, which, without a conscious effort on your part to seek diversion, may limit your life experience.

I have long believed that there are no accidents in life, but this personal experience confirmed this for me in a very profound way. I am grateful to my writers' retreat friends for their influence in this direction. Look into *your heart* and find the things that will ignite a passion for life in you. Frequent participation and regular involvement in those passions will be what truly brings balance into your life.

Help From The Experts

It's obviously true that there is no *magic pill, no quick-fix,* no one specific marketing idea that will catapult you to the top of your field. It takes a lot of planning, discipline, focus, and work. You will not achieve at a significant level without the dream, nor will the dream ever be realized without a strong work effort, and keeping a watchful eye on the goal plan. Here you can see your dream broken down into individual categories, then into the tiniest baby steps that must be taken each day toward the fulfillment of your greatness, as defined only by you.

You'll find it both comforting and reassuring to realize that there is a lot of very high quality help along the way. Don't be afraid to ask. It has continually been my experience that the people who are the most successful are consistently the most willing to help.

I have referenced many of my real-life heroes throughout this book. Many are so incredibly successful that they've achieved celebrity status and are in outrageously high demand as speakers, mentors, and trainers. Some now consult with huge corporations. Surprisingly, the good news for people like you and me, who value the opportunity to learn, is that they are all very approachable, and admirably human in their willingness to share and teach.

To make it easier for you to seek them out, The Mike Ferry Organization is in Newport Beach, California. So is Mark Victor Hansen; in fact he moved out there several years ago at Mike's urging. Howard Brinton's Star Power, Inc. is in Boulder, Colorado. Lauren Harper-Haden is with RE/MAX in North Hoffman Estates, Illinois. Dave Beson and David Knox are both in Minneapolis. For personal life coaching, Carol Adrienne's Spiral Path is in El Cerrito, California. Brian Tracy is in San Diego. All are on the Internet.

Contact these extraordinary people and seek their help. *This is what they do*. Mike, Howard, Lauren, Dave, and David are all real estate specific, and they're the Best of the Best. Carol can help you with the personal and spiritual areas of your life, and she can show you incredible insights and places to find joy you never knew existed. Mark and Brian can inspire you to greatness through the psychology of selling and the strength of your belief system. So find a mentor, maybe more than one, and do something toward formulating your *life plan*.

Then, be prepared to take the steps outlined in your plan and make them a part of you through internalization and dedicated repetition of the things you know work for you. Have a Master Mind alliance of some kind - the combining of at least one other creative mind like yours - at least one person close to you who will *always* support and encourage you.

Brad and I have long believed that a very significant part of the reason we've both had the good fortune of success in our respective fields is because we've always had each other as our Master Mind Partner. Together we've plotted, planned, dreamed, and schemed, and each of us has always said to the other, *"Go for it. You can do this."* He has helped me find a way to enter into long-term learning relationships with the great people who have taught me the best life lessons and helped me the most.

There really are no accidents in life. We are *always* put in the path of the people we need to meet, at the precise time we should meet them. The events of the last eleven years have proved that to me many, many times over, and I am enormously grateful for the amazing teachers and the incredible opportunities I have had.

It is my sincere hope that these ideas and systems, some of which I have followed to the letter, others that I've tweaked a bit here and there, which are compiled in this book, will help you achieve your goals and dreams, and will lead you to great happiness throughout your life's journey.

Acknowledgements:

I would like to thank the special people whose guidance and valued contributions made this book a reality: Mary Ann Carman, whose invitation led me to the Sedona Writers' Retreat, Carol Adrienne, whose enthusiastic nudge encouraged me to write it. Tom Bird, my writing mentor who guided me every step of the way, and especially to my editor, Jamie Saloff, who made it all come together. Special thanks to all of my teachers and mentors throughout my career who have helped me believe that truly, all things are possible.

About The Author

Sue Christensen is a 25-year veteran of the highly competitive and constantly changing real estate industry. She is a committed, life-long learner and prides herself in remaining open to new ideas.

Her personal secret to success is maintaining a steadfast focus on life's true priorities and her core values, while resisting the temptation to over-complicate her business.

Sue is an Associate Broker with RE/MAX Premier Realty in Tucson, Arizona, and she conducts high-energy, hands-on workshops where she teaches life balance for the highly productive at all career levels.

A

ABC list, 31, 38, 40
Adrienne, Carol, 190
   Spiral Path, 190
affirmations, 11-13, 185, 187
   defined, 11
   recording on tape, 12
Albuquerque, 128
Arizona, 136, 138, 188
Arizona Association of Realtors, ix, 10
   Convention, ix, 10
assistant: See also delegation
   duties of, 104, 115
   job description, 68-71
Austin, 122

B

Bain, Del, 109, 128, 161, 162
Beson, Dave, x, 125, 189
Bird, Tom, 187
Boulder, 189
brain-storming: See Master Minding
Brinton, Howard, x, 30, 38, 46, 189
   Star Power, Inc, 189
Brokers, ix, 164
burn out, 47
Burton, Lance, 131
business planning, x, 11, 23-28, 142, 165
   desk fee, 102
   financial goals, 55
   florist, 115
   implementing ideas, 139
      prioritizing, 141
   market pricing, 100-101
   newsletter, 64
   number tracking, 55-57
   revenue-generating, 55, 172
   revenue-instigating, 55, 172
   staff compensation, 170
   stay focused, 170
   tracking your numbers, 25, 171
   where to begin, 24
   Why section, 185
Business Planning Program, 32-33
Buyer Agent, 54-55, 165
Buyer Specialist, 123

C

Cabela's, 178
California, 189, 190
Canfield, Jack, 9
cell phone, 158
   Money Line, 55, 102
   yard sign number, 55
Chamber Ambassador, 128, 137
Chamber Board of Directors, 137
Chamber of Commerce, 135, 137, 176
   New Member lunches, 128
Chicken Soup For The Soul, 9, 124
Cincinnati, 109
Clinton, Bill, 187
Colorado, 189
commission, 27, 90, 102, 162-165
   100%, 163, 164
   referral fees, 165
   traditional split, 27
contact management program, 86, 104, 117
   assistant's duties, 87
   follow-ups, 66
   Just Listed, 30
   Just Sold, 30
   neighbors, 30
contract presentation
   Counter Offer forms, 158
   faxing, 157
contracts, 107
conventions, 15-16, 130, 139
   national events, 18

D

delegation, 48-49, 61-83
   closings, 61
   colleagues, 151
   hiring an assistant, 66-67
      advertising for, 71
      check lists, 78
      commissions, 78
      desired characteristics, 67
      interviewing, 72-76
      job description, 68-71
      orientation, 76
      reviewing resumes, 71
      sphere of influence list, 76
      training, 78-82

when you need one, 67
letting go, 77
mindset with, 62
paper work, 61
personal chores, 153
Preferred Client Referral Form, 152
referrals, 151, 165
relocation Buyers, 150
servicing listings, 61
sign contractor, 155
training, 61
Diamond, Neil, 150, 151
Dillard's Department Store, 176
    Santa Hint Card, 177
Disney World, 18
door-knocking, 36
    ABC script, 38
    clues, 127
    how to, 37
    major employers, 40
    what to ask, 37, 39
    where to look, 37

E

El Cerrito, 190
expenses
    personal marketing, 27
Expireds, 30
    script for, 33-34

F

Ferry, Mike, ix, 9, 10, 17, 32, 36, 173, 186, 189
    five day week, 45-47
    Mike Ferry Organization, 189
Flagstaff, viii, ix, 9, 32, 35, 48, 123, 130, 136, 137, 146, 154, 176, 188
Flagstaff Mall, 50, 178
Flagstaff Symphony, 129
floor time, ix, 54
flyer box, 55
Forest Highlands, 96
FSBO, 30
    script for, 33-34

G

goal setting, 3-7, 185

business plan., 11
dreaming, 3
expectations, 185
Goal Planning Guide, 5
re-evaluation, 168
treasure map, 9
visualization, 9
written, 9
Graceland, 18

H

Hansen, Mark Victor, 9, 187, 189
Harper-Haden, Lauren, x, 189
    video programs, 49
Hawaii, 8
Hill, Napoleon, 13
housewarming gift, 116

I

Illinois, 189
interest rates, viii

J

JC Penny, 176, 178

K

Keillor's, Garrison, 8
Knox, David, x, 89, 105, 109, 189

L

Lake Woebegone, 8
Las Vegas, 131
League of Women Voters, 138
licensing, ix
life balance, x, 188
life script, 4
listings
    advertising, 90
    average sale price, 162
    backbone of business, 163
    Buyer Brokerage Agreement, 92
    Buyer Information form, 93
    Buyer Interview, 92
    Come List Me call, 63, 132, 133

Escrow File Check List, 81
floor agent, 102, 165
Just Listed cards, 106
Just Sold cards, 106
listing appointment, 56, 106-110
listing presentation, 25, 89-90
motivation, 91
New Listing Check List, 79
newsletter, 64
over-priced, 34-35
Pre-Listing Package, 105
qualifying, 90-91
    script for, 95
Seller's Homework form, 108
Twelve Important Questions, 106
lock box, 47-48

M

market analysis, 99-101
marketing, viii, 119, 139, 165
  CD ROM, 145
  client appreciation events, 119-124
    beach party, 123
    Christmas, 120
    Cookie Exchange, 122
    Easter Egg Hunt, 121
    Halloween party, 122
    Ice Cream Social, 121
    Newcomers' Club, 123
    wine and cheese, 122
    Winter Carnival, 123
  drawings, 131
  high-profile events, 131
  Little League, 137
  Neighborhood Services Directory, 134
  news column, 138
  newsletter, viii, 63, 122, 132
    contact information, 63
    costs, 63
    inserts, 63
    MLS data, 63, 132
    outsourcing, 63
    photographs, 122
    purpose, 64
    theme, 132
    when to mail, 65
    where to send, 65
  panic promotions, 140

personal brochure, viii
personal promotion, x, 127-138
  clothing, 127
  jewelry, 127
  Just Listed cards, 133
  Just Sold cards, 133
  logo, 128
  Meet Your New Neighbor cards, 133
  organizations, 127
  photos, 129-130
Professional Services Directory, 145
promotional campaign, 128-132
recognition, 134
rolling billboards, 141-145
  Humvee, 141
  moving van, 142
  PT Cruiser, 141
  tent, 145
  VW 'Bug', 141
theme, 128
Top Twelve System, 139-141
web site, 135
zero-based advertising, 145-146
Master Minding, 13, 15-20, 128, 130, 133, 190
  convention attendees, 16
  discussions, 16
  role-playing, 17
  video taping, 17
Memphis, 18
mentoring, viii, 189
  great mentors, x
mindset, vii-x, 3, 50, 172
  approval of others, 51-52
  available hours, 48
  beliefs and, 7
  customer satisfaction, 98
  daily routine, 10
  know yourself, 48
  life balance, 49
  of success, 187
  Open Houses, 51
  part of success formula, 9
  passion for life, 189
  professionalism, 151
  Queen of Self-Satisfaction, 188
  re-focus, 185
  referral-based business, 150
  resolving problems, 119
  serving heart element, 149

standards, 118
tapes for, 8, 173
under-promise, over-deliver, 109
with assistant, 62-63
Minneapolis, 190
Minnesota, 8
money
  attitudes about, 7
Multiple Listing Service (MLS), viii, 48, 55, 63, 64, 78, 88, 90, 99, 109, 110, 156, 163
  MLS Market Place Check List, 100

N

National Association of Realtors, viii
nay-sayers, 12, 15, 61
Newport Beach, 189
newsletter, 163: See marketing
  business generator, 163
Nightengale, Earl, 3
North Hoffman Estates, 189
Northern Arizona, 128

O

Open Houses, ix, 49-50
  alternative marketing, 54
  scripting, 53
Oprah, 17
Orlando, 18

P

personal time, x, 45-57, 158
  booked solid, 45
  boundaries, 49, 50, 51
  daily habits, 51
  days off, 52-57, 157
    Drop-everything-and-respond-list, 159
    exceptions, 158
    provisions for, 54
    scheduling, 55
    scripting, 53
    three principles, 52
  family time, 50
  five day week, 45
  life balance, 49
  referrals, 46
  scripting, 46

vacation, 49
Phoenix, ix, 16, 17, 46, 96, 130, 150, 186, 189
Preferred Buyer, 172
pricing, 109
  appraiser's role, 88
  price reduction, 89
  script for, 89
Pricing Your Home To Sell, 89, 109
Productivity School, 32
prospecting, ix, x
  a sacred appointment, 32
  ABC list, 31
  anybody you know, 30
  call sheet, 86
  daily log, 42
  determines production, vii
  disqualifying people, 35
  door-knocking, 36-40, 170
  Everybody I Know List, 35
  Expireds, 30, 171
  for appointments, 30
  FSBOs, 30, 171
  going three deep, 30
  high impact calls, 171
  Just Listed, 30
  Just Sold, 30
  lead follow-up calls, 104
  leads, definition for, 104
  Model Day, 56
  number per week, 103
  one hour a day, 31
  order to call, 33
  overview, 41
  practicing, 30
  pricing, 170
  reducing the amount of, 29
  referrals, 47
  scheduling, 101
  system, 85-87
  using the telephone to, 29
  what to ask, 30

R

real estate school, ix
Retail Sales
  extended customer service, 177
  Jewelry Broker, 175
  Jewelry Broker's Action Plan, 179

phone script for, 181
post card, 182
King of her Dreams, 176
Preferred Customer Program, 178
prospecting, 179
rookie, 161
rules, 47, 107, 124

S

safety precautions, 95-97
San Diego, 190
Scottsdale Fashion Square, 178
Sears, 176, 178
Sedona, 187
sign contractor, 155-156
six figure income, 47
   higher productivity, 154
   listings per month, 101
   one percent of the U.S. population, 138
   spending habits, 186
   system for, 159
   time frame, 101
   top priority, 66
sphere of influence, viii
State Department of Real Estate, 138
Success Secrets Of Self-Made Millionaires, 9
Superstar Retreat, 10, 32, 186
systems
   at home, 154
   color-coded, 87
   follow up system, 87-89, 117
   Letter Writer software, 125
   listings, 96
   pre-listing packages, 89
   prospecting system, 85
   purpose of, 85
   sign contractor, 155

T

taxes, 162, 186
Texas, 122
thank you notes, 20
   handwritten, 36
   referrals, 36
   Sellers, 115
   with a photo, 120
Tracy, Brian, 8, 9, 190

Treasure Mapping, 9-11, 18, 185, 187
   mini-treasure map, 10
Tucson, 16, 130

U

University of South Dakota, viii, 37, 39

V

Vermillion, viii, ix, 37, 38, 118

W

White Mountains, 17
work ethic: See mindset

Z

Ziglar, Zig, 7

Printed in the United States
6132